AUTOMATE
WITH PYTHON

100+ Recipes for Automating Daily Tasks

THOMPSON CARTER

TABLE OF CONTENTS

INTRODUCTION

The Power of Python in Everyday Automation

1. Why Automate? The Modern Need for Efficiency

- **Understanding Automation's Role Today**
  Describe how digital transformation and technological advancements have led to an era where efficiency and speed are paramount. Explain that automation is not just about eliminating repetitive tasks but enhancing productivity and creativity by freeing up time for more critical activities.

- **The Benefits of Automation**
  Outline the advantages, such as reduced human error, consistency, and scalability. Explain that automating tasks not only benefits individuals but can also streamline workflows in teams, businesses, and large-scale operations.

2. Why Python for Automation?

- **Python's Popularity and Versatility**
  Discuss Python's rise as a favorite language due to its readability, vast community support, and extensive libraries. Python's syntax is straightforward, making it ideal for beginners and advanced users alike. Its popularity spans

across various domains like data science, web development, and of course, automation.

- **Python Libraries That Make Automation Possible**
  Highlight key Python libraries that facilitate automation, such as os for operating system tasks, pandas for data manipulation, selenium for web automation, and smtplib for email automation. Introduce readers to the toolkit they will use throughout the book.

3. Understanding Python's Automation Potential in Everyday Scenarios

- **Breaking Down What Python Can Automate**
  Provide an overview of the types of tasks Python can automate—file handling, email management, data processing, web scraping, task scheduling, and more. Use real-world examples, such as automatically organizing files, managing spreadsheets, and sending periodic reports.
- **Applications in Personal Life, Work, and Business**
  Show readers how automation can improve aspects of daily life, from organizing a home photo library to tracking expenses, managing social media, and even home automation with IoT devices. For professionals, demonstrate how Python can handle repetitive tasks in project management, reporting, and data analysis.

4. A Tour of Python Automation Libraries
(600 words)

- **Introducing Libraries by Category**
  Group the libraries by task categories, like file management (os, shutil), web scraping (requests, BeautifulSoup, Selenium), data manipulation (pandas, numpy), and system monitoring (psutil). Explain the purpose of each library briefly to build familiarity.

- **How These Libraries Will Be Used Throughout the Book**
  Let readers know they'll have hands-on experience with each library through recipes designed to show practical use cases. Explain that by the end, they'll have a toolkit they can adapt for custom automation scripts.

5. Overview of the Book Structure

- **The Recipe-Based Approach**
  Explain that each chapter is structured as a set of recipes, with each recipe focused on a specific task. Readers can follow these recipes directly or use them as inspiration for building their own.

- **A Practical Guide for Every Skill Level**
  Emphasize that the book is intended for readers of all skill levels. While beginners will find the step-by-step guidance

useful, more advanced users will appreciate the breadth of applications and ideas for customizing scripts.

6. How to Use This Book

- **Tips   for   Beginners**
  Encourage beginners to start with simpler recipes and gradually work up to more complex scripts. Advise them to experiment by tweaking parameters to see how changes affect outcomes.

- **Customization and Adaptation for Advanced Users**
  Suggest that advanced users adapt the recipes by integrating them with other projects. Provide examples like combining multiple scripts for workflow automation, and offer tips on troubleshooting common issues.

- **Setting   Up   the   Development   Environment**
  Provide guidance on setting up Python, installing libraries, and using IDEs like PyCharm or VS Code. Include a brief section on using virtual environments to manage dependencies for different projects.

7. Ethics and Considerations in Automation
(600 words)

- **The Fine Line Between Efficiency and Overreach**
  Discuss ethical considerations around automation, especially in areas like web scraping or automating

interactions that might affect other people (e.g., social media or email automation). Emphasize the importance of using automation responsibly.

- **Avoiding Unintended Consequences**
Explain how poorly designed automation can lead to issues, like accidentally deleting files, spamming contacts, or misinterpreting data. Emphasize best practices, such as starting with small tests, using logging to track actions, and adding safeguards to prevent errors.

8. Case Studies: Real-World Impact of Python Automation

- **Small Businesses and Freelancers**
Provide examples of small businesses or freelancers who have used Python automation to handle client reports, social media, email outreach, and invoicing, saving time and reducing overhead.

- **Enterprise Applications**
Describe cases where Python automation has been used in enterprise environments to automate processes like data extraction, task scheduling, and real-time monitoring. Emphasize that Python is a scalable solution suitable for both individual and organizational needs.

9. What You'll Achieve by the End of This Book
(400 words)

- **Practical, Adaptable Skills**
  Assure readers that they'll finish the book with concrete skills for tackling daily tasks using Python, and they'll gain confidence in adapting scripts to suit their unique needs.

- **A Foundation for Further Exploration**
  Mention that mastering these recipes provides a foundation for more complex Python applications, from building full-scale applications to diving into specialized fields like data science, web development, or AI.

This comprehensive introduction will set the stage effectively by covering the relevance of Python automation, guiding readers through the necessary foundational knowledge, and previewing what they'll gain from each chapter in the book. This breakdown, once expanded, will offer both an inspiring start and a practical roadmap for readers to understand and embrace automation in their daily tasks.

CHAPTER 1: INTRODUCTION TO PYTHON AUTOMATION

In this chapter, we'll cover the essentials of Python automation, offering a broad understanding of what automation with Python entails, the tools required to set up an automation environment, and the key libraries that will be used throughout the book. This chapter provides a foundation for readers to begin their journey into automating repetitive tasks efficiently with Python.

1.1 Overview of Python for Automation

Python has become one of the most widely-used programming languages for automation, primarily due to its simplicity, readability, and an extensive ecosystem of libraries. Unlike other programming languages that may be more complex or specialized, Python's syntax is close to plain English, making it an ideal choice for automation, even for those with limited programming experience. Python's flexibility means it can be applied to almost any automation task, from simple file organization to complex web scraping and data management.

Why Python for Automation?
Python's popularity for automation stems from several unique advantages:

- **Easy to Learn**: Python's simple syntax allows beginners to pick it up quickly, and its clear, readable structure makes it ideal for writing and maintaining scripts.
- **Versatile Libraries**: Python has libraries tailored for nearly every type of task you could want to automate, from handling files and interacting with operating systems to automating browser actions and manipulating spreadsheets.
- **Cross-Platform Compatibility**: Python works seamlessly across Windows, Mac, and Linux, making it ideal for users on any platform.

In this book, we will explore Python's potential to save time by automating tedious tasks, improving both personal productivity and organizational workflows. Whether you're looking to organize files, send email alerts, scrape data from the web, or automate recurring tasks, Python provides a versatile toolkit for getting the job done.

1.2 Setting Up the Environment

To begin automating with Python, you need a properly configured development environment. This involves installing Python, setting up necessary libraries, and configuring an Integrated Development Environment (IDE) for easier coding and testing.

Installing Python

1. **Download and Install Python**: Python can be downloaded from python.org. Select the version compatible with your operating system (usually the latest stable version) and follow the instructions for installation.

2. **Configure Path Settings**: During installation, ensure you add Python to your system's PATH environment variable. This allows you to access Python commands directly from your command line or terminal.

Setting   Up   Virtual   Environments

Using virtual environments in Python is a good practice, especially when working on multiple automation projects with different dependencies. Virtual environments allow you to install libraries separately for each project, preventing conflicts between different versions of libraries.

1. **Create a Virtual Environment**:

   bash

   python -m venv automation_env

2. **Activate the Virtual Environment**:
   - On Windows: automation_env\Scripts\activate
   - On   macOS/Linux: source automation_env/bin/activate

3. **Install Libraries in the Virtual Environment**: Once activated, any libraries you install will be isolated within this environment.

Choosing   an   IDE

While Python scripts can be written in any text editor, using an IDE can streamline the development process. Popular options include:

- **VS Code**: Known for its versatility and extensive extensions.
- **PyCharm**: A dedicated Python IDE with powerful debugging and code navigation.
- **Jupyter Notebooks**: Ideal for testing small code snippets and visualizing outputs.

1.3 Key Libraries for Python Automation

Automation in Python is largely powered by libraries that offer pre-built methods and functions to handle a wide range of tasks. Here's an overview of some essential libraries that we will use throughout this book:

1. **os**

   The os library provides functions to interact with the operating system, making it invaluable for file and directory manipulation. Common tasks include listing files, creating directories, renaming files, and deleting unnecessary files.

Example Use Cases:

- o Organizing files based on types or dates
- o Renaming or deleting batches of files

Basic Syntax:

python

import os
os.listdir('path_to_directory') # Lists files in a directory
os.rename('old_filename', 'new_filename')   # Renames a file

2. **sys**

The sys library allows you to interact with the Python runtime environment, including access to command-line arguments, environment variables, and error handling.

Example Use Cases:

- o Managing input arguments for scripts
- o Modifying system settings within scripts

Basic Syntax:

python

```
import sys
sys.argv  # Command-line arguments list
sys.exit()  # Exits a script with a specified status
```

3. **shutil**

   shutil is designed for higher-level file operations, such as copying and moving files and directories. This library complements os by simplifying more complex file manipulations.

   Example Use Cases:

   - Backing up important files to a separate location
   - Creating automated archiving systems

   Basic Syntax:

   python

```
import shutil
shutil.copy('source_file', 'destination_directory')  # Copies a file
shutil.move('source_file', 'destination_directory')  # Moves a file
```

4. **schedule**

The schedule library allows you to run Python scripts at scheduled intervals, making it easy to automate tasks without relying on external schedulers like cron jobs.

Example Use Cases:

- o Running daily backups
- o Fetching data at regular intervals for reporting

Basic Syntax:

python

```
import schedule
import time

def job():
    print("Executing scheduled task...")

schedule.every().day.at("10:00").do(job)

while True:
    schedule.run_pending()
    time.sleep(1)
```

5. **pyautogui**

The pyautogui library automates keyboard and mouse actions, making it suitable for tasks that require interaction with GUI applications.

Example Use Cases:

o   Automating repetitive form submissions
o   Taking screenshots or triggering specific sequences on your desktop

Basic Syntax:

python

```
import pyautogui
pyautogui.click(x=100, y=200)   # Clicks at a specific
screen position
pyautogui.typewrite("Hello, World!") # Types text
```

These libraries form the backbone of most Python automation scripts. Throughout this book, we'll see how these libraries work in harmony to help you automate everything from organizing files and sending emails to managing social media and scraping data from the web. By the end of this chapter, you should have your environment set up and be ready to start working through practical recipes to automate a variety of tasks.

In this chapter, you learned why Python is an ideal language for automation, how to set up your environment, and gained a brief introduction to some of the key libraries that will power your automation projects. With this foundation, you are now ready to dive into specific recipes that address real-world tasks, helping you to become more efficient and productive by automating daily routines.

CHAPTER 2: FILE AND FOLDER MANAGEMENT

Managing files and folders is one of the most common and practical uses of Python automation. In this chapter, we'll explore how to automate tasks related to file creation, renaming, moving, organizing folders, handling duplicate files, and implementing backup systems. These recipes will save time and prevent manual errors, making it easier to maintain an organized digital workspace.

2.1 Automating File Creation, Renaming, and Moving

Handling files—creating, renaming, and moving them—is fundamental in almost any automation scenario. Python's os and shutil libraries provide straightforward functions for these tasks.

Automating File Creation

Creating files in specific formats or directories is often necessary when organizing data, initializing projects, or setting up templates.

Example Recipe: Creating Monthly Report Files
This script generates a new file for each month of the year in a specific directory, allowing for automated report file generation.

python

```python
import os

# Directory for storing reports
report_directory = 'reports'

# Ensure the directory exists
os.makedirs(report_directory, exist_ok=True)

# Create report files for each month
for month in range(1, 13):
    filename = f'{report_directory}/report_{month:02d}.txt'
    with open(filename, 'w') as file:
        file.write(f'Report for month {month}\n')
```

```python
print(f'Created {filename}')
```

Renaming Files in Bulk

Automating file renaming can help in situations where files have inconsistent or unstructured names. With Python, we can easily rename files based on patterns or prefixes.

Example Recipe: Renaming Photos Based on a Timestamp
This script renames all .jpg files in a folder to include a timestamp, making them easier to organize.

python

```python
import os
import time

photo_directory = 'photos'

for filename in os.listdir(photo_directory):
    if filename.endswith('.jpg'):
        new_name                                          =
f"{time.strftime('%Y%m%d_%H%M%S')}_{filename}"
        os.rename(f"{photo_directory}/{filename}",
f"{photo_directory}/{new_name}")
        print(f'Renamed {filename} to {new_name}')
```

Moving Files to Specified Folders

Moving files to appropriate folders is useful for organizing data by category, type, or date.

Example Recipe: Organizing Documents by File Type This script organizes files into folders based on their file types, making it easy to find and access specific file categories.

python

```python
import os
import shutil

source_directory = 'documents'
destination_directories = {
    'pdf': 'pdfs',
    'docx': 'word_docs',
    'xlsx': 'excel_files'
}

for filename in os.listdir(source_directory):
    file_extension = filename.split('.')[-1]
    if file_extension in destination_directories:
        dest_folder = destination_directories[file_extension]
        os.makedirs(dest_folder, exist_ok=True)
        shutil.move(f"{source_directory}/{filename}",
f"{dest_folder}/{filename}")
```

```
print(f'Moved {filename} to {dest_folder}')
```

2.2 Organizing Folders and Handling Duplicates

Folder organization involves more than moving files; it often includes creating, sorting, and managing folder structures to avoid clutter. Duplicate files, on the other hand, can take up unnecessary space and cause confusion. Python can help automate folder organization and duplicate file handling.

Automating Folder Structure Creation

For larger projects, setting up a standardized folder structure can be beneficial. Here's a script to automate that process.

Example Recipe: Creating a Project Folder Structure
This script sets up a basic folder structure for a new project, with folders for documents, images, data, and scripts.

python

```python
import os

project_name = 'new_project'
folders = ['documents', 'images', 'data', 'scripts']

for folder in folders:
    path = f"{project_name}/{folder}"
    os.makedirs(path, exist_ok=True)
```

```
print(f'Created folder: {path}')
```

Identifying and Removing Duplicate Files

Duplicate files can arise from downloading the same files multiple times or creating unnecessary copies. Python can identify duplicates by checking file sizes, file names, or even hash values.

Example Recipe: Detecting Duplicate Files by File Hash This script identifies duplicate files in a directory based on their hash values and provides an option to delete them.

python

```python
import os
import hashlib

def file_hash(filename):
    hasher = hashlib.md5()
    with open(filename, 'rb') as file:
        buf = file.read()
        hasher.update(buf)
    return hasher.hexdigest()

duplicates = {}
directory = 'target_folder'

for filename in os.listdir(directory):
```

```
filepath = f"{directory}/{filename}"
file_hash_value = file_hash(filepath)
if file_hash_value in duplicates:
    print(f"Duplicate     found:     {filename}     (same     as
{duplicates[file_hash_value]})")
    # Uncomment below to delete duplicate
    # os.remove(filepath)
else:
    duplicates[file_hash_value] = filename
```

2.3 Backing Up and Restoring Files

Backups are crucial to prevent data loss. Automation ensures that files are backed up consistently and systematically. This section explores creating backups and restoring them when needed.

Automating Backups

Creating backups typically involves copying files from the main directory to a backup location. We'll use the shutil library to automate this process.

Example Recipe: Daily Backup of Important Files This script copies essential files to a backup directory, timestamping each backup for easy retrieval.

python

```python
import os
import shutil
from datetime import datetime

source_directory = 'important_files'
backup_directory = 'backups'

# Create a timestamped backup folder
backup_folder = f"{backup_directory}/backup_{datetime.now().strftime('%Y%m%d_%H%M%S')}"
os.makedirs(backup_folder, exist_ok=True)

for filename in os.listdir(source_directory):
    shutil.copy(f"{source_directory}/{filename}", f"{backup_folder}/{filename}")
    print(f'Backed up {filename} to {backup_folder}')
```

Restoring Files from Backup

If data is lost or corrupted, backups allow you to restore the files quickly.

Example Recipe: Restoring the Latest Backup
This script restores the latest backup by copying files from the most recent backup directory to the main directory.

python

27

```
import os
import shutil

backup_directory = 'backups'
main_directory = 'important_files'

# Find the latest backup folder
latest_backup = sorted(os.listdir(backup_directory))[-1]
latest_backup_path = f"{backup_directory}/{latest_backup}"

for filename in os.listdir(latest_backup_path):
    shutil.copy(f"{latest_backup_path}/{filename}",
f"{main_directory}/{filename}")
    print(f'Restored {filename} from backup')
```

In this chapter, you learned how to automate essential file and folder management tasks, such as creating, renaming, and moving files, organizing folder structures, detecting and handling duplicates, and implementing a backup system. These foundational techniques not only simplify file management but also improve data organization and security, providing a solid base for future automation tasks. The next chapter will build on this by delving into web scraping and data gathering automation techniques.

CHAPTER 3: AUTOMATING WEB SCRAPING

Web scraping is a powerful technique for extracting and processing data from websites. Automating web scraping can transform how you collect information, making it easy to gather data continuously, update databases, monitor trends, and extract insights. In this chapter, we'll explore how to use Python libraries such as BeautifulSoup and requests to extract data, employ

Selenium for interactive web scraping tasks, and set up scheduled scrapers to run at regular intervals.

3.1 Using BeautifulSoup and Requests to Gather Data

BeautifulSoup and requests are two core libraries in Python used for web scraping. While requests handles the process of sending HTTP requests and receiving the content from a web page, BeautifulSoup makes it easy to parse the HTML and locate the specific data you're interested in.

Setting Up the Environment

Before diving into the code, install the necessary libraries:

bash

pip install requests beautifulsoup4

Basic Web Scraping with BeautifulSoup and Requests

To get started, let's look at a simple example of using requests and BeautifulSoup to fetch data from a static website and parse it for specific information.

Example Recipe: Scraping Titles of Articles from a Blog
In this example, we'll fetch a webpage containing blog posts and extract the titles of the articles.

python

```
import requests
from bs4 import BeautifulSoup

# URL of the webpage to scrape
url = "https://example-blog.com/articles"

# Send a request to the webpage
response = requests.get(url)

# Parse the HTML content with BeautifulSoup
soup = BeautifulSoup(response.text, 'html.parser')

# Find and print all article titles
for title in soup.find_all('h2', class_='article-title'):
    print(title.get_text())
```

This script sends a GET request to the blog page and parses the response using BeautifulSoup. It then finds all <h2> tags with a specific class, retrieves the text, and displays each article title.

Extracting Data from Complex HTML Structures

Sometimes, the data you need is nested within multiple HTML tags or has attributes like id or class that make it easier to locate. Understanding the HTML structure of the page you're scraping is essential.

Example Recipe: Scraping Product Information from an E-commerce   Site
This script scrapes product names and prices from an e-commerce webpage, capturing structured data for each product.

python

```python
import requests
from bs4 import BeautifulSoup

url = "https://example-ecommerce.com/products"
response = requests.get(url)
soup = BeautifulSoup(response.text, 'html.parser')

products = []
for product in soup.find_all('div', class_='product-item'):
    name = product.find('h3', class_='product-name').get_text()
    price = product.find('span', class_='product-price').get_text()
    products.append({'name': name, 'price': price})

for product in products:
    print(product)
```

In this example, BeautifulSoup parses nested HTML tags to retrieve specific elements, allowing you to gather structured data from the site.

3.2 Automating Web Interactions with Selenium

For websites that require user interaction (e.g., clicking buttons, filling out forms, navigating dynamically loaded content), Selenium is the preferred tool. Unlike requests and BeautifulSoup, which work well on static pages, Selenium can interact with elements on dynamic websites.

Setting Up Selenium

To use Selenium, you'll need to install the library and download a WebDriver (e.g., ChromeDriver for Chrome, GeckoDriver for Firefox).

bash

```
pip install selenium
```

Then, download the appropriate WebDriver, place it in a directory, and specify its path when initializing Selenium in your code.

Interacting with Web Pages Using Selenium

Example Recipe: Logging into a Website and Extracting Data
Here, we'll use Selenium to log into a website, navigate to a specific page, and extract data that's only accessible after logging in.

python

```
from selenium import webdriver
```

```python
from selenium.webdriver.common.by import By
from selenium.webdriver.common.keys import Keys
import time

# Set up the WebDriver (replace with the path to your WebDriver)
driver = webdriver.Chrome(executable_path='path/to/chromedriver')

# Open the website and log in
driver.get("https://example-login.com")
username_field = driver.find_element(By.ID, "username")
password_field = driver.find_element(By.ID, "password")

username_field.send_keys("your_username")
password_field.send_keys("your_password")
password_field.send_keys(Keys.RETURN)

# Wait for the page to load
time.sleep(5)

# Navigate to a data page and scrape information
driver.get("https://example-login.com/data-page")
data_elements = driver.find_elements(By.CLASS_NAME, "data-class")
```

```
for element in data_elements:
    print(element.text)
```

```
# Close the driver
driver.quit()
```

In this example, Selenium automates the process of logging in by entering credentials and pressing Enter. After logging in, it navigates to another page and extracts specific data elements.

Automating Dynamic Content Interactions

Websites that load content dynamically (e.g., using JavaScript) can be handled by simulating interactions such as scrolling, clicking "Load More" buttons, or expanding elements.

Example Recipe: Scrolling to Load More Content
Many social media sites or forums load content as you scroll. This script automates scrolling to load more content and scrape it.

python

```
from selenium import webdriver
import time
```

```
driver = webdriver.Chrome(executable_path='path/to/chromedriver')
driver.get("https://example-scroll.com")
```

```python
# Scroll down to load more content
last_height                =                driver.execute_script("return
document.body.scrollHeight")
while True:
    driver.execute_script("window.scrollTo(0,
document.body.scrollHeight);")
    time.sleep(3)  # Wait for new content to load
    new_height             =                driver.execute_script("return
document.body.scrollHeight")
    if new_height == last_height:
        break
    last_height = new_height


# Extract content once fully loaded
content_elements    =    driver.find_elements(By.CLASS_NAME,
"content-class")
for element in content_elements:
    print(element.text)


driver.quit()
```

This script scrolls down the page in intervals, waiting for content to load, until it reaches the end of the page. It then extracts the desired data.

3.3 Scheduling Regular Web Scraping Tasks

Once your web scraping scripts are working, you may want them to run at regular intervals to keep data up-to-date. Python's schedule library makes it easy to set up automated tasks.

Installing the schedule Library

Install the schedule library:

bash

```
pip install schedule
```

Scheduling a Web Scraper to Run Daily

The following script demonstrates how to schedule a web scraping task to run daily at a specific time.

Example Recipe: Running a Daily News Scraper
This script scrapes headlines from a news site every day at a specified time.

python

```
import schedule
import time
import requests
from bs4 import BeautifulSoup


def scrape_headlines():
```

```
url = "https://example-news.com"
response = requests.get(url)
soup = BeautifulSoup(response.text, 'html.parser')
headlines    =    [headline.get_text()    for    headline    in
soup.find_all('h1', class_='headline')]

for headline in headlines:
    print(headline)


# Schedule the scraper to run daily at 8:00 AM
schedule.every().day.at("08:00").do(scrape_headlines)


while True:
    schedule.run_pending()
    time.sleep(1)
```

Here, the schedule library runs scrape_headlines every day at 8:00 AM. The loop keeps the script running, checking every second if a scheduled task is due. This approach ensures regular, hands-free data collection.

In this chapter, you learned the essentials of web scraping with Python. Using requests and BeautifulSoup, you can gather data from static pages, while Selenium enables interactions with dynamic websites. Finally, you saw how to schedule your web scraping tasks to run automatically, ensuring your data stays updated with minimal effort. As you move forward, remember to respect website terms of service and scraping ethics. In the next chapter, we'll cover automation techniques for managing emails, enhancing productivity further by automating your communications.

CHAPTER 4: WORKING WITH EMAILS

Managing emails is one of the most common and time-consuming tasks in personal and professional settings. Automating email interactions using Python can help you filter, organize, send, and retrieve important information without manual intervention. In this chapter, we'll explore how to automate email reading and filtering, send emails with attachments, and integrate with popular email providers like Gmail using their APIs.

4.1 Automating Email Reading and Filtering

Automating email reading and filtering can be particularly useful for sorting incoming messages, identifying priority emails, or moving specific messages to designated folders. Python's imaplib library is typically used to interact with IMAP email accounts, allowing you to connect to the server, search emails, and retrieve them for processing.

Setting Up Email Access with IMAP

To begin, ensure that your email provider allows IMAP access. For Gmail, you need to enable "IMAP Access" under Gmail's settings. If you're using two-factor authentication, you may need to generate an app-specific password.

Basic Script for Accessing Emails

Here's a simple script to connect to an email account using IMAP, search for emails by subject, and retrieve their contents.

python

```
import imaplib
import email
```

```python
from email.header import import decode_header

# Email account credentials
username = "your_email@example.com"
password = "your_password"

# Connect to the IMAP server
mail = imaplib.IMAP4_SSL("imap.gmail.com")
mail.login(username, password)

# Select the inbox folder
mail.select("inbox")

# Search for emails with a specific subject
status, messages = mail.search(None, 'SUBJECT "Important"')
email_ids = messages[0].split()

# Fetch and print each email's subject
for email_id in email_ids:
    status, msg_data = mail.fetch(email_id, "(RFC822)")
    for response_part in msg_data:
        if isinstance(response_part, tuple):
            msg = email.message_from_bytes(response_part[1])
            subject, encoding = decode_header(msg["Subject"])[0]
            if isinstance(subject, bytes):
```

```
        subject = subject.decode(encoding or "utf-8")
    print("Subject:", subject)
```

mail.logout()

In this script, we connect to Gmail using imaplib, select the inbox, search for emails with "Important" in the subject, and print out the subject of each email.

Filtering Emails Based on Conditions

You can filter emails based on other criteria, like the sender or specific keywords in the subject or body. This example script retrieves unread emails and checks for a keyword in the body of the email.

Example Recipe: Filtering Unread Emails with a Keyword

python

```
import imaplib
import email

# Connect and login as in previous example
mail.select("inbox")

# Search for unread emails
status, messages = mail.search(None, 'UNSEEN')
email_ids = messages[0].split()
```

```python
# Check each unread email for a specific keyword in the body
for email_id in email_ids:
    status, msg_data = mail.fetch(email_id, "(RFC822)")
    for response_part in msg_data:
        if isinstance(response_part, tuple):
            msg = email.message_from_bytes(response_part[1])
            if msg.is_multipart():
                for part in msg.walk():
                    if part.get_content_type() == "text/plain":
                        body = part.get_payload(decode=True).decode()
                        if "urgent" in body.lower():
                            print("Found an urgent email:", msg["Subject"])
                            break
```

This code fetches unread emails, checks the body for the word "urgent," and prints the subject if found.

4.2 Sending Emails with Attachments

Python's smtplib library allows you to send emails, while the email library helps you create and structure the email content. Sending emails with attachments can be helpful for automated reporting, sharing files, or notifications.

Basic Email Sending

This basic example demonstrates how to send a plain text email using SMTP.

python

```python
import smtplib
from email.message import EmailMessage

# Email details
sender = "your_email@example.com"
recipient = "recipient_email@example.com"
subject = "Automated Email"
body = "This is an automated message."

# Set up the email
msg = EmailMessage()
msg.set_content(body)
msg["Subject"] = subject
msg["From"] = sender
msg["To"] = recipient

# Send the email
with smtplib.SMTP_SSL("smtp.gmail.com", 465) as smtp:
    smtp.login(sender, "your_password")
    smtp.send_message(msg)
```

```python
print("Email sent successfully.")
```

Sending Emails with Attachments

Sending Emails with Attachments

To send an email with an attachment, add the file to the email as a MIME part. This example script sends a message with a PDF file attached.

Example Recipe: Sending an Email with a PDF Attachment

python

```python
import smtplib
from email.message import EmailMessage

sender = "your_email@example.com"
recipient = "recipient_email@example.com"
subject = "Monthly Report"
body = "Please find the attached monthly report."

# Create the email
msg = EmailMessage()
msg.set_content(body)
msg["Subject"] = subject
msg["From"] = sender
msg["To"] = recipient

# Attach a file
```

```
file_path = "report.pdf"
with open(file_path, "rb") as file:
    file_data = file.read()
    file_name = file_path.split("/")[-1]
    msg.add_attachment(file_data,          maintype="application",
subtype="pdf", filename=file_name)


# Send the email with SMTP
with smtplib.SMTP_SSL("smtp.gmail.com", 465) as smtp:
    smtp.login(sender, "your_password")
    smtp.send_message(msg)


print("Email with attachment sent successfully.")
```

This code creates an email with a subject, body, and a PDF attachment, then sends it through Gmail's SMTP server.

4.3 Integrating Python with Popular Email Providers (e.g., Gmail API)

For more advanced email automation, such as accessing Gmail without IMAP or handling more complex email interactions, you can use the Gmail API. This API provides more features than standard IMAP, like secure access and integration with other Google services.

Setting Up the Gmail API

To access Gmail through the API, you'll need to set up a Google Cloud project and enable the Gmail API:

1. Go to Google Cloud Console.
2. Create a new project and enable the Gmail API.
3. Create OAuth credentials and download the credentials.json file.
4. Install the Google client libraries:

bash

```
pip install --upgrade google-auth google-auth-oauthlib google-auth-httplib2 google-api-python-client
```

Authenticating and Accessing Emails with Gmail API

Example Recipe: Authenticating and Reading Unread Emails

This script authenticates with Gmail API and retrieves unread emails.

python

```
from google.oauth2 import service_account
from googleapiclient.discovery import build
import base64
import email
```

```
# Authenticate with service account credentials
SCOPES = ['https://www.googleapis.com/auth/gmail.readonly']
creds                                                      =
service_account.Credentials.from_service_account_file('credential
s.json', scopes=SCOPES)
service = build('gmail', 'v1', credentials=creds)


# Retrieve unread emails
results        =        service.users().messages().list(userId='me',
q='is:unread').execute()
messages = results.get('messages', [])


for msg in messages:
    msg_data      =      service.users().messages().get(userId='me',
id=msg['id']).execute()
    msg_str                                                =
base64.urlsafe_b64decode(msg_data['raw'].encode('ASCII')).decod
e('utf-8')
    msg_obj = email.message_from_string(msg_str)
    print("Subject:", msg_obj["Subject"])
```

This script authenticates with Gmail's API, retrieves unread emails, and displays their subjects.

Sending Emails with Gmail API

The Gmail API also allows sending emails, which can be beneficial for automated notifications, reminders, or scheduled emails.

Example Recipe: Sending an Email with Gmail API

python

```python
import base64
from google.oauth2 import service_account
from googleapiclient.discovery import build
from email.mime.text import MIMEText

def create_message(sender, to, subject, message_text):
    message = MIMEText(message_text)
    message['to'] = to
    message['from'] = sender
    message['subject'] = subject
    raw = base64.urlsafe_b64encode(message.as_bytes()).decode()
    return {'raw': raw}

# Authenticate with Gmail API
SCOPES = ['https://www.googleapis.com/auth/gmail.send']
creds = service_account.Credentials.from_service_account_file('credentials.json', scopes=SCOPES)
```

```
service = build('gmail', 'v1', credentials=creds)

# Create and send email
message       =        create_message("your_email@example.com",
"recipient_email@example.com", "Test Subject", "Hello, this is a
test.")
sent          =           service.users().messages().send(userId="me",
body=message).execute()
print("Message sent successfully:", sent)
```

This code snippet creates a MIME email message and sends it through the Gmail API, providing a secure way to automate email sending without using SMTP credentials directly.

In this chapter, we explored how to automate email-related tasks using Python. We covered reading and filtering emails with imaplib, sending emails with smtplib, and using the Gmail API for more robust and secure email management. Automating email interactions can streamline communication, improve productivity, and provide a more efficient way to handle important messages. In the next chapter, we'll move to data collection and parsing automation techniques, delving deeper into Python's ability to handle various data sources and formats.

CHAPTER 5: AUTOMATING DATA COLLECTION AND PARSING

In many applications, data collection and parsing are critical tasks that support decision-making, analysis, and automation. Python offers powerful tools to handle data in various formats, including JSON, CSV, and XML. Additionally, Python makes it easy to interact with APIs for fetching data from external sources and automate the insertion and updating of this data in databases. This chapter will cover how to automate these tasks, parse data from different formats, and perform database updates.

5.1 Working with JSON, CSV, and XML Data Formats

Python's standard libraries provide convenient tools for reading, writing, and parsing JSON, CSV, and XML data formats, each suited to different types of data storage and exchange.

JSON (JavaScript Object Notation)

JSON is a lightweight data-interchange format often used for APIs and configuration files. Python's json library allows for easy reading and writing of JSON data.

Example Recipe: Parsing JSON Data from a File

Here's an example of how to load and parse JSON data from a file.

python

```
import json
```

```
# Load JSON data from a file
```

```
with open("data.json", "r") as file:
    data = json.load(file)

# Access data fields
for entry in data["items"]:
    print(f"Name: {entry['name']}, Price: {entry['price']}")
```

This script reads a JSON file, parses it, and prints specific fields from each item. JSON data is especially useful for hierarchical data structures, where nested elements can represent more complex data.

CSV (Comma-Separated Values)

CSV is a simple text format that stores tabular data. Python's csv library provides tools to read and write CSV files, which are commonly used for data imports, exports, and spreadsheets.

Example Recipe: Automating Data Entry into a CSV File

Let's say you want to log daily data into a CSV file. This script appends a new row to a CSV file each time it's run.

python

```
import csv
from datetime import datetime

# Data to append
```

```python
new_data = ["Item A", 12.99, datetime.now().strftime("%Y-%m-%d %H:%M")]
```

```python
# Append data to CSV file
with open("log.csv", "a", newline="") as file:
    writer = csv.writer(file)
    writer.writerow(new_data)
```

```python
print("Data appended to log.csv")
```

This script appends a row with a timestamp to an existing CSV file, making it easy to automate logging tasks.

XML (Extensible Markup Language)

XML is a widely-used format for structured data, especially in enterprise systems. Python's xml.etree.ElementTree library provides tools to parse and manipulate XML files.

Example Recipe: Parsing XML Data from a File

In this example, we'll parse an XML file containing product information.

python

```python
import xml.etree.ElementTree as ET
```

```python
# Load XML data from a file
```

```
tree = ET.parse("products.xml")
root = tree.getroot()

# Iterate through products and print details
for product in root.findall("product"):
    name = product.find("name").text
    price = product.find("price").text
    print(f"Name: {name}, Price: {price}")
```

This script parses an XML file, retrieves each product's name and price, and prints them. XML parsing is useful when working with structured data from complex systems like inventory management or billing.

5.2 Fetching Data from APIs

APIs (Application Programming Interfaces) allow applications to interact with external data sources or services. Many websites and applications provide public APIs to access their data programmatically. Python's requests library is ideal for making HTTP requests to APIs.

Setting Up the Requests Library

If not already installed, install requests via pip:

bash

```
pip install requests
```

Making Basic API Requests

Here's a basic example of using requests to fetch data from a public API.

Example Recipe: Fetching Weather Data from an API

This script fetches the current weather for a specified city using the OpenWeather API.

python

```python
import requests

api_key = "your_api_key"
city = "London"
url = f"http://api.openweathermap.org/data/2.5/weather?q={city}&appid={api_key}"

# Send GET request to the API
response = requests.get(url)
data = response.json()

# Extract and print weather information
temperature = data["main"]["temp"]
```

description = data["weather"][0]["description"]

print(f"The temperature in {city} is {temperature}°K with {description}")

This code sends a request to the OpenWeather API and parses the response to display the temperature and weather description.

Automating API Calls and Handling Responses

To handle regular data updates, automate API calls by storing the retrieved data in a file or database. You can also set up a scheduled job to make periodic requests.

Example Recipe: Fetching and Storing Stock Price Data

This script fetches stock price data from a financial API and saves it in a CSV file.

python

```
import requests
import csv
from datetime import datetime

# API URL and parameters
api_key = "your_api_key"
symbol = "AAPL"
```

```
url =
f"https://financialmodelingprep.com/api/v3/quote/{symbol}?apike
y={api_key}"

# Fetch data from API
response = requests.get(url)
data = response.json()[0]  # Assuming API returns a list with one
item

# Prepare data for CSV
row = [data["symbol"], data["price"],
datetime.now().strftime("%Y-%m-%d %H:%M")]

# Append to CSV file
with open("stock_prices.csv", "a", newline="") as file:
    writer = csv.writer(file)
    writer.writerow(row)

print(f"Stock data for {symbol} saved.")
```

This script fetches stock prices and appends them to a CSV file, making it easy to track historical price changes over time.

5.3 Automating Database Updates and Data Parsing

Automating database updates is beneficial for applications that require regular data refreshes, like dashboards, inventory systems, or customer relationship management (CRM) tools. Python's sqlite3 library is great for local databases, while SQLAlchemy can be used for more robust database management.

Setting Up and Inserting Data into a Database

We'll use SQLite in this example to create a database, define a table, and insert data programmatically.

Example Recipe: Creating and Populating a SQLite Database

This script creates a database for customer information, adds a new customer, and prints all entries.

python

```python
import sqlite3

# Connect to SQLite database (or create it if it doesn't exist)
conn = sqlite3.connect("customers.db")
cursor = conn.cursor()

# Create a table for customer data
cursor.execute("""
CREATE TABLE IF NOT EXISTS customers (
    id INTEGER PRIMARY KEY AUTOINCREMENT,
    name TEXT NOT NULL,
    email TEXT NOT NULL,
    joined_date TEXT NOT NULL
```

```
)
""")
```

```python
# Insert a new customer record
cursor.execute("INSERT   INTO   customers   (name,   email,
joined_date) VALUES (?, ?, ?)",
        ("John Doe", "john.doe@example.com", "2023-05-14"))
```

```python
# Commit changes and fetch all customer records
conn.commit()
cursor.execute("SELECT * FROM customers")
rows = cursor.fetchall()
```

```python
# Print customer records
for row in rows:
    print(row)
```

```python
# Close the connection
conn.close()
```

This script creates a table for customer data, inserts a record, and retrieves all records from the table.

Automating Data Parsing and Updates

You can combine API requests with database updates to automate data fetching and storage, which is useful for real-time dashboards or reports.

Example Recipe: Updating a Database with Weather Data

This example fetches weather data from an API and stores it in a database table for historical tracking.

python

```python
import requests
import sqlite3
from datetime import datetime

# Database connection
conn = sqlite3.connect("weather.db")
cursor = conn.cursor()

# Create table for weather data
cursor.execute("""
CREATE TABLE IF NOT EXISTS weather (
    id INTEGER PRIMARY KEY AUTOINCREMENT,
    city TEXT,
    temperature REAL,
    description TEXT,
    date_time TEXT
)
""")
```

```python
# Fetch data from weather API
api_key = "your_api_key"
city = "London"
url = f"http://api.openweathermap.org/data/2.5/weather?q={city}&appid={api_key}"
response = requests.get(url)
data = response.json()

# Prepare data and insert into the database
temperature = data["main"]["temp"]
description = data["weather"][0]["description"]
date_time = datetime.now().strftime("%Y-%m-%d %H:%M")

cursor.execute("INSERT INTO weather (city, temperature, description, date_time) VALUES (?, ?, ?, ?)",
        (city, temperature, description, date_time))

# Commit changes and close connection
conn.commit()
print(f"Weather data for {city} saved.")
conn.close()
```

This script automates the process of fetching weather data and storing it in a database table, creating a log of historical weather data for analysis or reporting.

In this chapter, we covered various methods of data collection and parsing, focusing on JSON, CSV, and XML formats. We explored how to fetch data from APIs, process it, and save it to files or databases. Finally, we examined how to automate database updates to manage data efficiently and programmatically. These skills are essential for building data-driven applications and automating workflows that depend on external or internal data sources. Next, we'll move on to task scheduling to learn how to automate the execution of scripts and workflows at predefined intervals.

CHAPTER 6: TASK SCHEDULING

Automating repetitive tasks on a schedule is essential for workflows that require periodic updates, data collection, backups, or report generation. This chapter will cover setting up scheduled tasks on different operating systems using cron jobs (Linux/macOS) and Task Scheduler (Windows). We'll also explore Python libraries like schedule and APScheduler, which allow for programmatic scheduling within Python scripts, and provide recipes for designing daily, weekly, or monthly tasks.

6.1 Setting Up Automated Tasks with Cron Jobs and Task Scheduler

On Linux and macOS, cron jobs are used to schedule tasks at specified intervals, while on Windows, Task Scheduler performs a similar function. Let's look at how to set up tasks using both methods.

Cron Jobs (Linux/macOS)

Cron is a command-line utility in Unix-like systems that executes commands or scripts automatically at specific times and intervals.

Basic   Cron   Syntax

Cron jobs are defined in a crontab file, with each line specifying a command to execute. The general syntax for scheduling a job in cron is:

plaintext

* * * * * command_to_run

Each asterisk corresponds to a time unit in the following order:

- Minute (0–59)
- Hour (0–23)
- Day of the month (1–31)
- Month (1–12)
- Day of the week (0–6, Sunday=0)

Example Recipe: Setting Up a Daily Cron Job

Suppose you have a Python script backup.py that you want to run every day at midnight. To set this up as a cron job:

1. Open your crontab file:

bash

```
crontab -e
```

2. Add the following line:

bash

```
0 0 * * * /usr/bin/python3 /path/to/backup.py
```

This job will run backup.py daily at midnight. Save and exit the editor to activate the cron job.

Task Scheduler (Windows)

On Windows, Task Scheduler provides a graphical interface for scheduling tasks, as well as command-line options through PowerShell.

Example Recipe: Scheduling a Script with Task Scheduler

1. Open **Task Scheduler** and select **Create Basic Task....**
2. Set a name for the task, such as "Daily Backup," and click **Next**.
3. Choose the frequency (e.g., Daily) and set the time for the task.
4. Select **Start a Program** as the action.
5. Browse to the path of your Python executable (e.g., python.exe) and add the path to your script (e.g., backup.py) in the arguments section.
6. Click **Finish** to save and activate the task.

With Task Scheduler, you can automate running your Python scripts at any interval you need.

6.2 Using the schedule and APScheduler Libraries

If you prefer handling scheduling within Python rather than relying on the OS, schedule and APScheduler are two Python libraries that offer scheduling capabilities directly in your code. This can be useful for cross-platform applications, as it simplifies the scheduling process and makes it easier to manage tasks from within Python scripts.

The schedule Library

Schedule is a simple library that lets you set up tasks at specific intervals, such as every hour, daily, or weekly. It's ideal for lightweight scheduling needs within a Python script.

Installing schedule

bash

pip install schedule

Example Recipe: Running a Daily Task with schedule

Let's say you want to automate a daily report generation at 9:00 AM.

python

```
import schedule
import time

def generate_report():
    print("Generating daily report...")
```

```python
# Schedule the task to run daily at 9:00 AM
schedule.every().day.at("09:00").do(generate_report)

# Run the scheduler
while True:
    schedule.run_pending()
    time.sleep(1)
```

This script will run the generate_report function daily at 9:00 AM. The while loop checks if any tasks are scheduled to run and executes them.

Example Recipe: Running a Task Every Hour

You can also set up tasks to run on an hourly basis or any other interval.

python

```python
def hourly_task():
    print("Running hourly task...")


schedule.every().hour.do(hourly_task)

while True:
    schedule.run_pending()
    time.sleep(1)
```

This example sets up an hourly task. Using schedule for short intervals works well, but it may not be ideal for complex scheduling needs, which is where APScheduler comes in.

The APScheduler Library

APScheduler (Advanced Python Scheduler) provides more advanced scheduling options, including cron-like scheduling, background execution, and better control over intervals.

Installing APScheduler

bash

pip install apscheduler

Example Recipe: Running a Job with Cron Scheduling in APScheduler

This example sets up a cron-style job to run every Monday at 8:30 AM.

python

from apscheduler.schedulers.blocking import BlockingScheduler

def weekly_task():
    print("Running weekly task...")

scheduler = BlockingScheduler()

scheduler.add_job(weekly_task, 'cron', day_of_week='mon', hour=8, minute=30)

scheduler.start()

This script uses BlockingScheduler to keep the scheduler active. The cron parameters (day_of_week, hour, and minute) control when the task runs.

Example Recipe: Running a Task Every 10 Minutes with APScheduler

For more granular control over time intervals, APScheduler allows setting intervals in minutes, hours, or days.

python

```
from apscheduler.schedulers.blocking import BlockingScheduler

def task():
    print("Running task every 10 minutes...")


scheduler = BlockingScheduler()
scheduler.add_job(task, 'interval', minutes=10)
scheduler.start()
```

This code schedules a task to run every 10 minutes, using interval to set the time between executions.

6.3 Designing Scripts for Daily, Weekly, or Monthly Tasks

When designing scripts to run at regular intervals, consider the types of tasks you want to automate, such as backups, data collection, or report generation. Here are examples of scripts designed for daily, weekly, and monthly automation tasks.

Daily Task: Data Collection and Backup

Suppose you want to collect data from an API and back it up daily at 7:00 AM. This can be achieved with the schedule library.

python

```python
import schedule
import time
import requests
import json
from datetime import datetime

def collect_and_backup_data():
    print("Collecting and backing up data...")
    response = requests.get("https://api.example.com/data")
    data = response.json()

    # Save data to a JSON file with a timestamp
```

```python
    with
open(f"backup_{datetime.now().strftime('%Y%m%d')}.json",
"w") as file:
        json.dump(data, file)


schedule.every().day.at("07:00").do(collect_and_backup_data)

while True:
    schedule.run_pending()
    time.sleep(1)
```

This script collects data from an API and saves it to a JSON file with a timestamp every day at 7:00 AM.

Weekly Task: Generating a Report

Weekly tasks can be useful for report generation or summaries. This example uses APScheduler to generate a report every Friday at 5:00 PM.

python

```python
from apscheduler.schedulers.blocking import BlockingScheduler

def weekly_report():
    print("Generating weekly report...")

scheduler = BlockingScheduler()
```

```
scheduler.add_job(weekly_report, 'cron', day_of_week='fri',
hour=17)
scheduler.start()
```

This task runs every Friday at 5:00 PM, generating a report or summary.

Monthly Task: Data Archiving

For tasks that only need to run monthly, such as archiving old data, use APScheduler with a monthly interval.

python

```python
from apscheduler.schedulers.blocking import BlockingScheduler
import shutil

def archive_data():
    print("Archiving data for the month...")

shutil.make_archive(f"archive_{datetime.now().strftime('%Y%m')
}", 'zip', 'data_directory')

scheduler = BlockingScheduler()
scheduler.add_job(archive_data, 'cron', day=1, hour=0, minute=0)
# Runs on the first day of the month
scheduler.start()
```

This script creates an archive of a directory on the first day of each month at midnight, which is useful for end-of-month data retention or backups.

In this chapter, you learned how to automate task scheduling across different platforms. We covered setting up cron jobs on Linux/macOS, using Task Scheduler on Windows, and leveraging schedule and APScheduler libraries within Python scripts. Finally, we explored examples for designing daily, weekly, and monthly tasks, such as data collection, report generation, and data archiving. In the next chapter, we'll look at text and document processing automation to manage files and extract meaningful insights.

CHAPTER 7: AUTOMATING TEXT AND DOCUMENT PROCESSING

Automating text and document processing can save significant time, especially when handling repetitive tasks like reading, writing, editing text files, processing PDFs, and extracting text from scanned documents. Python offers robust tools for each of these tasks, enabling efficient handling of large volumes of text and document data. In this chapter, we'll cover how to automate text file operations, work with PDFs, and use Optical Character Recognition (OCR) for text extraction from images.

7.1 Working with Text Files: Reading, Writing, and Editing

Text files are commonly used for logs, configuration files, data storage, and documentation. Automating the reading, writing, and editing of text files can simplify tasks like data entry, report generation, and data cleaning.

Reading Text Files

Reading text files in Python is straightforward with the open() function. You can read the file's content as a whole, line-by-line, or even selectively based on specific conditions.

Example Recipe: Reading a Log File and Extracting Errors

This script reads a log file and extracts lines that contain error messages.

python

```python
# Open the log file in read mode
with open("system.log", "r") as file:
    lines = file.readlines()

# Filter for lines containing "ERROR"
error_lines = [line for line in lines if "ERROR" in line]

for error in error_lines:
    print(error.strip())
```

This code reads each line from the file, filters for lines with the keyword "ERROR," and prints them. Such a script is useful for quickly identifying issues in log files.

Writing to Text Files

Python can create new files or append data to existing files, which is useful for logging, report generation, or configuration management.

Example Recipe: Writing a Summary Report to a Text File

This script generates a summary report from data and saves it to a text file.

python

```python
data = [
    {"name": "John Doe", "score": 85},
    {"name": "Jane Smith", "score": 92},
    {"name": "Bob Johnson", "score": 78},
]

# Open a file in write mode
with open("summary_report.txt", "w") as file:
    file.write("Summary Report\n")
    file.write("==============\n")
    for entry in data:
        file.write(f"Name: {entry['name']}, Score: {entry['score']}\n")

print("Report saved to summary_report.txt")
```

This script creates a summary report file and writes each entry from the data list to the file.

Editing Text Files

Editing files programmatically allows for batch modifications, such as updating configuration files or formatting logs.

Example Recipe: Replacing Keywords in a Configuration File

This script reads a configuration file, replaces a keyword, and saves the changes.

python

```
# Load and modify configuration file
with open("config.txt", "r") as file:
    content = file.read()

# Replace a placeholder with a new value
content = content.replace("PLACEHOLDER", "new_value")

# Save the modified content
with open("config.txt", "w") as file:
    file.write(content)

print("Configuration updated.")
```

This code replaces all occurrences of "PLACEHOLDER" in config.txt with "new_value," automating the process of updating configuration settings.

7.2 Automating PDF Processing

PDFs are a standard format for documents, but they can be challenging to work with programmatically. Python's PyPDF2 and pdfplumber libraries allow for reading, merging, splitting, and extracting text from PDF files.

Setting Up PDF Libraries

Install PyPDF2 and pdfplumber:

bash

pip install PyPDF2 pdfplumber

Reading and Extracting Text from PDFs

PyPDF2 provides a simple way to extract text from PDF pages, which is useful for text analysis, reporting, or data extraction.

Example Recipe: Extracting Text from a PDF Document

This script extracts text from each page in a PDF file.

python

```python
import PyPDF2

# Open PDF file
with open("document.pdf", "rb") as file:
    pdf_reader = PyPDF2.PdfReader(file)

    # Extract text from each page
    for page_num, page in enumerate(pdf_reader.pages):
        text = page.extract_text()
        print(f"Page {page_num + 1}:\n{text}\n")
```

This code opens a PDF file, extracts text from each page, and prints it.

Merging and Splitting PDFs

Automating PDF merging and splitting is useful for document management, especially when dealing with multi-page reports or file bundling.

Example Recipe: Merging Multiple PDF Files

This script merges multiple PDF files into one document.

python

```python
from PyPDF2 import PdfMerger

# List of PDF files to merge
pdf_files = ["file1.pdf", "file2.pdf", "file3.pdf"]

# Initialize PDF merger
merger = PdfMerger()

# Add each PDF file to the merger
for pdf in pdf_files:
    merger.append(pdf)

# Save the merged PDF
with open("merged_document.pdf", "wb") as output_file:
    merger.write(output_file)

print("PDF files merged into merged_document.pdf")
```

This script combines multiple PDFs into a single document, which can streamline document management tasks.

Extracting Specific Pages from a PDF

You can also automate the extraction of specific pages from a PDF.

Example Recipe: Extracting Pages from a PDF

This example extracts specific pages from a PDF and saves them as a new file.

python

```
from PyPDF2 import PdfWriter, PdfReader

input_pdf = "document.pdf"
output_pdf = "extracted_pages.pdf"

reader = PdfReader(input_pdf)
writer = PdfWriter()

# Add specific pages (e.g., 1 and 3)
for page_num in [0, 2]:  # Zero-indexed
    writer.add_page(reader.pages[page_num])

# Save the extracted pages to a new PDF
with open(output_pdf, "wb") as output_file:
```

```
writer.write(output_file)
```

```
print("Pages extracted to extracted_pages.pdf")
```

This script saves specific pages as a new PDF, which is useful for creating customized document subsets.

7.3 Extracting Text from Documents with OCR

OCR (Optical Character Recognition) allows you to extract text from images and scanned documents. Python's pytesseract library, which relies on Tesseract OCR, is commonly used for this purpose.

Setting Up OCR with Tesseract

To use OCR, install pytesseract and Tesseract. First, install Tesseract:

- On Ubuntu: sudo apt install tesseract-ocr
- On macOS (with Homebrew): brew install tesseract
- On Windows: Download the Tesseract installer and add it to your PATH.

Then, install pytesseract:

bash

pip install pytesseract

Basic OCR with pytesseract

pytesseract converts images into text, which is useful for processing scanned documents or images of text.

Example Recipe: Extracting Text from an Image

This script reads an image file and extracts text from it.

python

```
import pytesseract
from PIL import Image

# Load image
image = Image.open("scanned_document.png")

# Perform OCR
text = pytesseract.image_to_string(image)

print("Extracted Text:")
print(text)
```

This script uses pytesseract to extract text from a scanned image file. It's a convenient way to automate the processing of scanned documents.

Batch Processing Multiple Images

Automating OCR for multiple images can save time when working with large volumes of scanned documents.

Example Recipe: Batch OCR for Multiple Images in a Folder

This script performs OCR on all image files in a folder and saves the extracted text to individual files.

python

```python
import pytesseract
from PIL import Image
import os

# Folder containing images
image_folder = "scanned_docs"
output_folder = "extracted_text"

# Ensure the output folder exists
os.makedirs(output_folder, exist_ok=True)

# Process each image in the folder
for filename in os.listdir(image_folder):
    if filename.endswith(".png") or filename.endswith(".jpg"):
        image_path = os.path.join(image_folder, filename)
        image = Image.open(image_path)

        # Extract text with OCR
        text = pytesseract.image_to_string(image)
```

```
# Save extracted text to a file
output_path = os.path.join(output_folder, f"{filename}.txt")
with open(output_path, "w") as text_file:
    text_file.write(text)

print(f"Extracted text from {filename} to {output_path}")
```

This code iterates through all images in a folder, applies OCR to each image, and saves the extracted text to separate text files.

In this chapter, you learned how to automate text and document processing tasks, including working with text files, reading and writing PDFs, merging and splitting PDF files, and extracting text from scanned documents with OCR. These automation techniques are highly valuable for streamlining document management and data extraction, especially when dealing with large volumes of text-based data. In the next chapter, we'll cover data cleaning and formatting to help prepare data for analysis, reporting, and further automation.

CHAPTER 8: DATA CLEANING AND FORMATTING

Data cleaning and formatting are essential steps in data processing, as they ensure the data's accuracy, consistency, and usability. Without proper cleaning, data can produce misleading results, cause errors in automated workflows, and reduce overall efficiency. In this chapter, we'll cover how to handle missing data, duplicates, and inconsistencies, automate formatting for dates, currency, and units, and create reusable data-cleaning functions to streamline these tasks.

8.1 Handling Missing Data, Duplicates, and Inconsistencies

Real-world data often has missing values, duplicate records, and inconsistencies that need to be addressed before analysis or further processing. Python's pandas library offers powerful tools to identify and handle these issues.

Setting Up pandas

Install pandas if it isn't already installed:

bash

pip install pandas

Identifying and Handling Missing Data

Missing data is a common issue that can distort analysis and cause errors. The approach to handling missing data depends on the specific use case: you might fill in missing values, drop rows with missing values, or use a placeholder.

Example Recipe: Filling Missing Values

This script fills missing values with the median for numeric columns and a placeholder for text columns.

python

```python
import pandas as pd

# Sample data
data = {
    "Name": ["Alice", "Bob", "Charlie", None],
    "Age": [25, None, 30, 22],
    "City": ["New York", "Los Angeles", None, "Chicago"]
}
df = pd.DataFrame(data)

# Fill missing numeric values with the median
df["Age"].fillna(df["Age"].median(), inplace=True)

# Fill missing text values with a placeholder
```

```python
df["Name"].fillna("Unknown", inplace=True)
df["City"].fillna("Unknown", inplace=True)


print("Data after filling missing values:")
print(df)
```

This code replaces missing numeric values with the median and missing text values with a placeholder. This approach prevents empty data fields and ensures consistency.

Removing Duplicates

Duplicate records can skew data analysis and affect automated systems. pandas makes it easy to identify and remove duplicates.

Example Recipe: Removing Duplicate Rows

This script checks for duplicate rows and removes them from the DataFrame.

python

```python
# Sample data with duplicates
data = {
    "Name": ["Alice", "Bob", "Charlie", "Alice"],
    "Age": [25, 30, 30, 25],
    "City": ["New York", "Los Angeles", "Chicago", "New York"]
}
df = pd.DataFrame(data)
```

```python
# Remove duplicates based on all columns
df.drop_duplicates(inplace=True)
```

```python
print("Data after removing duplicates:")
print(df)
```

This code removes duplicate rows by identifying records with the same values in all columns. You can also specify specific columns to check for duplicates if needed.

Handling Inconsistent Data

Data inconsistencies, such as varying capitalization, different formats for dates, or multiple units for measurements, can make analysis challenging.

Example Recipe: Standardizing Text Data

This script standardizes text data by converting names to lowercase and trimming whitespace.

python

```python
data = {
    "Name": [" Alice ", "BOB", "Charlie ", "alice"],
    "Age": [25, 30, 30, 22],
    "City": ["New York", "Los Angeles", "Chicago", "New york"]
}
```

```
df = pd.DataFrame(data)

# Standardize text columns
df["Name"] = df["Name"].str.strip().str.lower()
df["City"] = df["City"].str.title()  # Capitalize each word

print("Data after standardizing text:")
print(df)
```

This script removes extra spaces and standardizes names to lowercase and cities to title case, creating a more consistent dataset.

8.2 Automating Data Formatting (Date, Currency, Units)

Automating data formatting ensures that data conforms to a standard structure, making it easier to use across different systems and analyses. Dates, currency, and measurement units often require specific formatting, especially when integrating data from various sources.

Formatting Dates

Dates may come in different formats or even as text. Converting them to a standard format (e.g., YYYY-MM-DD) allows for easier sorting, filtering, and analysis.

Example Recipe: Converting Date Formats

This script converts dates in different formats to a standard format (YYYY-MM-DD).

python

```python
data = {
    "Name": ["Alice", "Bob", "Charlie"],
    "Join Date": ["01/02/2021", "Feb 5, 2021", "2021-03-15"]
}
df = pd.DataFrame(data)

# Convert dates to a standard format
df["Join Date"] = pd.to_datetime(df["Join Date"])

print("Data with standardized dates:")
print(df)
```

This code uses pd.to_datetime() to parse different date formats and convert them to a standardized format.

Formatting Currency

Currency values are often represented in different formats or symbols. Standardizing these values as numeric data makes them easier to analyze.

Example Recipe: Cleaning and Formatting Currency Data

This script removes currency symbols and formats values as floats.

python

```
data = {
    "Item": ["Product A", "Product B", "Product C"],
    "Price": ["$1,200.50", "€900.30", "$750"]
}
df = pd.DataFrame(data)

# Remove symbols and commas, convert to float
df["Price"]    =    df["Price"].replace({'\$':    ",    '€':    "},
regex=True).replace({',': "}, regex=True).astype(float)

print("Data with formatted currency values:")
print(df)
```

This code removes currency symbols and commas, then converts prices to a numeric format.

Converting Units

Standardizing units (e.g., from inches to centimeters or pounds to kilograms) is useful for comparing measurements consistently.

Example Recipe: Converting Measurement Units

This script converts a column of values from inches to centimeters.

python

```
data = {
    "Item": ["Product A", "Product B", "Product C"],
```

91

```
    "Height (inches)": [12, 15, 10]
}
df = pd.DataFrame(data)

# Convert inches to centimeters
df["Height (cm)"] = df["Height (inches)"] * 2.54

print("Data with converted units:")
print(df)
```

This code creates a new column for height in centimeters by converting values from inches.

8.3 Creating Reusable Data Cleaning Functions

Reusable functions for data cleaning can streamline repetitive cleaning tasks, improve code organization, and make it easy to apply consistent cleaning steps across different datasets.

Creating a Function for Missing Data Handling

You can create a reusable function that fills missing values based on column types, making it adaptable to different datasets.

Example Recipe: Reusable Function for Handling Missing Data

This function fills missing values based on data type, using median for numeric columns and a placeholder for strings.

python

```python
def fill_missing_values(df, placeholder="Unknown"):
    for column in df.columns:
        if df[column].dtype == "object":
            df[column].fillna(placeholder, inplace=True)
        else:
            df[column].fillna(df[column].median(), inplace=True)
    return df


# Sample data
data = {
    "Name": ["Alice", None, "Charlie"],
    "Age": [25, None, 30],
    "City": [None, "Los Angeles", "Chicago"]
}
df = pd.DataFrame(data)


# Apply the function
df = fill_missing_values(df)
print(df)
```

This function identifies the data type of each column and fills missing values accordingly, which can save time when working with multiple datasets.

Creating a Function for Data Standardization

A function for standardizing text data can make it easy to apply consistent formatting across different datasets.

Example Recipe: Reusable Function for Standardizing Text Data

This function standardizes text columns by removing extra spaces and converting text to lowercase or title case as needed.

python

```python
def standardize_text_columns(df, columns):
    for column in columns:
        df[column] = df[column].str.strip().str.lower()
    return df

# Sample data
data = {
    "Name": [" Alice ", "BOB", "Charlie "],
    "City": ["New york", "los angeles", "CHICAGO"]
}
df = pd.DataFrame(data)

# Apply the function
df = standardize_text_columns(df, ["Name", "City"])
print(df)
```

This function removes leading/trailing spaces and standardizes text to lowercase, making it easier to achieve consistency in text data.

Creating a Function for Date Formatting

A reusable function for date formatting can convert date columns to a standard format across datasets.

Example Recipe: Reusable Function for Converting Date Columns

This function converts specified columns to a standard date format (YYYY-MM-DD).

python

```python
def standardize_date_columns(df, date_columns):
    for column in date_columns:
        df[column] = pd.to_datetime(df[column], errors="coerce")
    return df

# Sample data
data = {
    "Name": ["Alice", "Bob"],
    "Join Date": ["01/02/2021", "2021-03-15"]
}
df = pd.DataFrame(data)

# Apply the function
df = standardize_date_columns(df, ["Join Date"])
print(df)
```

This function converts date columns to a consistent format, handling various date inputs and any invalid dates as NaT (not a time).

In this chapter, you learned how to handle common data issues such as missing values, duplicates, and inconsistencies, automate data formatting for dates, currency, and units, and create reusable functions to streamline data-cleaning tasks. These techniques improve data quality, making it more accurate and consistent for analysis or automation. In the next chapter, we'll move on to automating report generation, leveraging clean and formatted data to produce insights efficiently.

CHAPTER 9: AUTOMATING REPORT GENERATION

Generating reports is a routine yet essential task in many fields, from business and finance to research and data analytics. Automating report generation can save significant time, especially for tasks that require regular updates or standard reporting formats. In this chapter, we'll cover how to automate the generation of Excel and CSV reports, create visual reports using Python's matplotlib and seaborn libraries, and integrate these reporting functions with email to deliver reports on a scheduled basis.

9.1 Generating Excel and CSV Reports

Python's pandas library is ideal for creating and exporting data reports in Excel and CSV formats. These formats are widely used, easy to handle, and compatible with many reporting and data analysis tools.

Creating CSV Reports

CSV is a simple format that's great for storing tabular data. Automating CSV exports makes it easy to generate raw data reports for various applications.

Example Recipe: Generating a Sales Report in CSV

This script generates a CSV report from sales data, making it easy to track monthly sales and share with stakeholders.

python

```python
import pandas as pd

# Sample sales data
data = {
    "Date": ["2023-01-01", "2023-01-02", "2023-01-03"],
    "Product": ["Widget A", "Widget B", "Widget A"],
    "Quantity": [10, 5, 8],
    "Revenue": [100, 50, 80]
}
df = pd.DataFrame(data)

# Export data to CSV
df.to_csv("sales_report.csv", index=False)
print("Sales report saved to sales_report.csv")
```

This script creates a simple CSV report containing daily sales records, which can be shared or imported into other systems for further analysis.

Creating Excel Reports

Excel reports allow for more complex formatting and can contain multiple sheets, which is beneficial for detailed reports. Python's pandas library, combined with openpyxl, can generate and style Excel files.

Example Recipe: Generating a Multi-Sheet Excel Report

This example creates a multi-sheet Excel report with summary and detailed data sections.

python

```python
import pandas as pd

# Sample data for different sheets
summary_data = {
    "Metric": ["Total Sales", "Average Revenue"],
    "Value": [300, 75]
}
detailed_data = {
    "Date": ["2023-01-01", "2023-01-02", "2023-01-03"],
    "Product": ["Widget A", "Widget B", "Widget A"],
```

```
    "Quantity": [10, 5, 8],
    "Revenue": [100, 50, 80]
}

# Create DataFrames
summary_df = pd.DataFrame(summary_data)
detailed_df = pd.DataFrame(detailed_data)

# Write data to Excel with multiple sheets
with pd.ExcelWriter("monthly_report.xlsx") as writer:
    summary_df.to_excel(writer,          sheet_name="Summary",
index=False)
    detailed_df.to_excel(writer,          sheet_name="Details",
index=False)

print("Excel report saved to monthly_report.xlsx")
```

This script generates an Excel report with two sheets—one for summary metrics and another for detailed data.

Formatting Excel Reports with openpyxl

Using openpyxl, you can add custom formatting to Excel reports, making them more visually appealing and easier to read.

Example Recipe: Adding Formatting to an Excel Report

In this script, we apply formatting to highlight headers and add cell colors to make the report easier to interpret.

python

```python
from openpyxl import Workbook
from openpyxl.styles import Font, PatternFill

# Create workbook and add data
wb = Workbook()
ws = wb.active
ws.title = "Sales Report"
data = [
    ["Date", "Product", "Quantity", "Revenue"],
    ["2023-01-01", "Widget A", 10, 100],
    ["2023-01-02", "Widget B", 5, 50]
]
for row in data:
    ws.append(row)

# Apply formatting to headers
header_fill                =                PatternFill(start_color="FFFF00",
end_color="FFFF00", fill_type="solid")
for cell in ws[1]:
    cell.font = Font(bold=True)
    cell.fill = header_fill

wb.save("formatted_sales_report.xlsx")
```

```
print("Formatted        Excel        report        saved        to
formatted_sales_report.xlsx")
```

This code highlights headers in yellow and bolds the font for emphasis, making the report more readable.

9.2 Automating Visual Reports with matplotlib and seaborn

Visual reports provide a quick way to interpret data and are particularly useful in presentations or dashboards. Python's matplotlib and seaborn libraries allow for creating customized visualizations that can be automated and saved to image files.

Setting Up matplotlib and seaborn

Install matplotlib and seaborn if they aren't already installed:

bash

```
pip install matplotlib seaborn
```

Creating Basic Visualizations

Example Recipe: Generating a Sales Bar Chart

This script creates a bar chart of monthly sales, providing an easy-to-read summary of performance.

python

```
import pandas as pd
import matplotlib.pyplot as plt
```

```
# Sample data
data = {
    "Month": ["January", "February", "March"],
    "Sales": [1500, 2000, 1800]
}
df = pd.DataFrame(data)

# Create bar chart
plt.figure(figsize=(8, 6))
plt.bar(df["Month"], df["Sales"], color="skyblue")
plt.xlabel("Month")
plt.ylabel("Sales")
plt.title("Monthly Sales")
plt.savefig("monthly_sales_chart.png")
plt.show()
```

This script generates a bar chart of monthly sales and saves it as an image file. This chart can be integrated into reports or presentations.

Creating More Complex Visualizations with seaborn

seaborn provides additional styles and visualization options, making it easier to create aesthetically pleasing charts.

Example Recipe: Generating a Line Plot with seaborn

This example uses seaborn to create a line plot showing trends in revenue over time.

python

```
import seaborn as sns

# Sample data
data = {
    "Date": pd.date_range(start="2023-01-01", periods=10),
    "Revenue": [200, 220, 215, 230, 225, 240, 250, 245, 255, 260]
}
df = pd.DataFrame(data)

# Create line plot
plt.figure(figsize=(10, 6))
sns.lineplot(x="Date", y="Revenue", data=df, marker="o")
plt.xlabel("Date")
plt.ylabel("Revenue")
plt.title("Revenue Trend Over Time")
plt.xticks(rotation=45)
plt.tight_layout()
plt.savefig("revenue_trend_chart.png")
plt.show()
```

This line plot tracks revenue over time, offering a clear view of performance trends. Saving it as an image allows for easy integration into reports.

9.3 Integrating Reporting Functions with Email for Regular Updates

Automating report generation and sending via email can streamline workflows, ensuring stakeholders receive regular updates without manual intervention. Python's smtplib and email libraries make it easy to send emails with attachments.

Sending Reports via Email

This example demonstrates how to send a report as an attachment in an automated email.

Example Recipe: Sending an Excel Report via Email

python

```
import smtplib
from email.message import EmailMessage

# Email details
sender = "your_email@example.com"
recipient = "recipient_email@example.com"
subject = "Monthly Sales Report"
body = "Please find attached the latest monthly sales report."
```

```python
# Create the email message
msg = EmailMessage()
msg["From"] = sender
msg["To"] = recipient
msg["Subject"] = subject
msg.set_content(body)


# Attach the Excel report
with open("monthly_report.xlsx", "rb") as file:
    report_data = file.read()
    msg.add_attachment(report_data,        maintype="application",
subtype="xlsx", filename="monthly_report.xlsx")


# Send the email
with smtplib.SMTP_SSL("smtp.gmail.com", 465) as smtp:
    smtp.login(sender, "your_password")
    smtp.send_message(msg)


print("Monthly report sent successfully.")
```

This script attaches the generated Excel report to an email and sends it to a specified recipient, which is useful for delivering regular updates.

Scheduling Automated Report Generation and Delivery

Combining data collection, report generation, and email delivery can automate the entire reporting process. Using Python's schedule library, you can run this process at specified intervals.

Example Recipe: Scheduling a Daily Report Delivery

In this example, we schedule the report generation and email sending process to run every day at a specified time.

python

```
import schedule
import time

def generate_and_send_report():
    # Data generation (sample data here)
    data = {"Date": ["2023-01-01", "2023-01-02"], "Sales": [100, 150]}
    df = pd.DataFrame(data)
    df.to_excel("daily_sales_report.xlsx", index=False)

    # Email details
    sender = "your_email@example.com"
    recipient = "recipient_email@example.com"
    subject = "Daily Sales Report"
    body = "Attached is the daily sales report."
```

```python
    msg = EmailMessage()
    msg["From"] = sender
    msg["To"] = recipient
    msg["Subject"] = subject
    msg.set_content(body)

    with open("daily_sales_report.xlsx", "rb") as file:
        report_data = file.read()
        msg.add_attachment(report_data,      maintype="application",
subtype="xlsx", filename="daily_sales_report.xlsx")

    # Send the email
    with smtplib.SMTP_SSL("smtp.gmail.com", 465) as smtp:
        smtp.login(sender, "your_password")
        smtp.send_message(msg)

    print("Daily report generated and sent.")

# Schedule the function to run daily at 8:00 AM
schedule.every().day.at("08:00").do(generate_and_send_report)

while True:
    schedule.run_pending()
    time.sleep(1)
```

This script schedules the generate_and_send_report function to run daily at 8:00 AM, automating the report generation and delivery.

In this chapter, you learned how to automate the creation of Excel and CSV reports, generate visual reports using matplotlib and seaborn, and integrate reporting functions with email for automated delivery. These techniques streamline reporting workflows, enabling you to share regular updates with minimal manual effort. In the next chapter, we'll explore task tracking and to-do list automation, helping you further manage workflows and deadlines effectively.

CHAPTER 10: BROWSER AUTOMATION AND WEB TESTING

Browser automation is invaluable for tasks that involve web interaction, such as form submissions, data extraction, account management, and repetitive tasks. Using Python's Selenium library, you can control the browser to perform these actions automatically. Additionally, Selenium is a powerful tool for automated web testing, allowing you to simulate user interactions and verify web application functionality. In this chapter, we'll cover how to control the browser with Selenium, automate repetitive browser tasks, and set up automated web tests in Python.

10.1 Controlling the Browser with Selenium

Selenium is a widely used library for browser automation. It supports most browsers and provides full control over web elements, enabling you to perform actions like clicking, typing, and navigating through pages.

Setting Up Selenium and WebDriver

To use Selenium, you need to install the selenium library and a WebDriver compatible with your browser (e.g., ChromeDriver for Chrome, GeckoDriver for Firefox).

Installation Instructions:

1. Install Selenium:

   bash

   pip install selenium

2. Download a WebDriver:
   - For Chrome, download ChromeDriver.
   - For Firefox, download GeckoDriver.
3. Ensure the WebDriver is accessible from your PATH or specify its location in your code.

Launching a Browser and Navigating Pages

The first step in browser automation is to launch the browser and navigate to a web page. Here's a basic example of launching Chrome and opening a website.

Example Recipe: Opening a Web Page with Selenium

python

```python
from selenium import webdriver

# Initialize WebDriver
driver = webdriver.Chrome(executable_path='path/to/chromedriver')

# Open a web page
driver.get("https://www.example.com")

print("Title:", driver.title)

# Close the browser
driver.quit()
```

This script launches Chrome, navigates to https://www.example.com, prints the page title, and closes the browser. The driver.get() method opens a URL, and driver.quit() closes the browser.

10.2 Automating Repetitive Browser Tasks

Automating repetitive tasks, such as form filling, button clicking, and data entry, is one of the primary uses of Selenium. Let's look at some examples of automating typical interactions.

Filling Forms Automatically

Many applications require form submissions, such as user registration or feedback forms. Selenium can automate this by locating input fields and sending text.

Example Recipe: Automating Form Filling

This script fills in a login form and submits it.

python

```
from selenium import webdriver
from selenium.webdriver.common.by import By
from selenium.webdriver.common.keys import Keys
import time

# Initialize WebDriver
driver = webdriver.Chrome(executable_path='path/to/chromedriver')
driver.get("https://www.example.com/login")

# Find and fill the username and password fields
```

```python
username_field = driver.find_element(By.ID, "username")
password_field = driver.find_element(By.ID, "password")


username_field.send_keys("your_username")
password_field.send_keys("your_password")


# Submit the form
password_field.send_keys(Keys.RETURN)


time.sleep(3)  # Wait for the page to load
print("Logged in successfully.")


driver.quit()
```

This code locates fields by their ID, inputs login credentials, and submits the form. You can adjust the find_element method to use other selectors (e.g., By.CLASS_NAME, By.XPATH) depending on the element's structure.

Clicking Buttons and Navigating Pages

Selenium can simulate clicks on buttons, links, or other clickable elements. This is useful for tasks like navigating through multi-page forms or e-commerce checkouts.

Example Recipe: Navigating Through Pages by Clicking Buttons

This script demonstrates navigating a multi-page form by clicking a "Next" button until a final page is reached.

python

```python
from selenium import webdriver
from selenium.webdriver.common.by import By
import time

# Initialize WebDriver
driver = webdriver.Chrome(executable_path='path/to/chromedriver')
driver.get("https://www.example.com/multi-step-form")

# Loop to click "Next" until the final page
while True:
    try:
        next_button = driver.find_element(By.ID, "next-button")
        next_button.click()
        time.sleep(2)  # Wait for the page to load
    except:
        print("Reached the final page.")
        break

driver.quit()
```

This code clicks the "Next" button until it encounters an exception (indicating the final page is reached). Automating navigation like this is useful for web forms or multi-step actions.

Automating Data Entry and Extraction

Selenium can handle both data entry and extraction, enabling you to input information and retrieve outputs, making it ideal for data collection and testing interactive applications.

Example Recipe: Automating Data Entry and Extracting Results

This example fills a search form, submits it, and retrieves results from the page.

python

```python
from selenium import webdriver
from selenium.webdriver.common.by import By
import time

# Initialize WebDriver
driver = webdriver.Chrome(executable_path='path/to/chromedriver')
driver.get("https://www.example.com/search")

# Enter a search query
search_field = driver.find_element(By.ID, "search-input")
search_field.send_keys("Python automation")
search_field.send_keys(Keys.RETURN)

# Wait for results to load and extract titles
```

```
time.sleep(3)
results = driver.find_elements(By.CLASS_NAME, "result-title")

for result in results:
    print(result.text)

driver.quit()
```

This code performs a search, waits for the results to load, and extracts titles from each search result. Such scripts can automate information retrieval for tasks like price monitoring or content aggregation.

10.3 Using Python for Automated Web Testing

Selenium is commonly used for automated web testing, which helps ensure that web applications behave as expected. Automated tests can check for functionality, layout consistency, and error handling.

Setting Up a Test with Assertions

Automated tests typically involve assertions to verify that the application behaves as expected. If an assertion fails, the test fails, which indicates that something in the application is not working correctly.

Example Recipe: Verifying Login Functionality with Assertions

This script tests a login form by verifying that the user is redirected to a dashboard page after logging in.

python

```python
from selenium import webdriver
from selenium.webdriver.common.by import By
from selenium.webdriver.common.keys import Keys
import time

driver = webdriver.Chrome(executable_path='path/to/chromedriver')
driver.get("https://www.example.com/login")

# Enter login credentials and submit
driver.find_element(By.ID, "username").send_keys("test_user")
driver.find_element(By.ID, "password").send_keys("test_password")
driver.find_element(By.ID, "password").send_keys(Keys.RETURN)

# Wait for redirection
time.sleep(3)

# Verify successful login by checking the URL
```

assert "dashboard" in driver.current_url, "Login failed: Dashboard not found in URL."

print("Login test passed.")

driver.quit()

This script automates a login test, checking if the URL contains "dashboard" after logging in. The assertion verifies that the user is redirected to the correct page, ensuring login functionality.

Testing Form Validations and Error Messages

Automated tests can verify that validation messages and error handling work as expected.

Example Recipe: Testing Form Validation for Required Fields

This example submits an incomplete form and checks for the appearance of an error message.

python

```
from selenium import webdriver
from selenium.webdriver.common.by import By
import time

driver =
webdriver.Chrome(executable_path='path/to/chromedriver')
driver.get("https://www.example.com/signup")
```

```
# Attempt to submit form without filling required fields
submit_button = driver.find_element(By.ID, "submit-button")
submit_button.click()

# Wait for error message to appear
time.sleep(2)

# Check for error message
error_message = driver.find_element(By.ID, "error-message")
assert error_message.is_displayed(), "Validation error message did
not appear."

print("Form validation test passed.")
driver.quit()
```

This script verifies that an error message appears when the form is submitted without required fields, ensuring that form validation is working correctly.

End-to-End Testing with Selenium

End-to-end tests simulate complete user workflows, such as a user journey through a shopping cart from login to checkout.

Example Recipe: Testing a Checkout Process

This test automates the entire checkout process, verifying each step from adding items to completing the purchase.

python

```python
from selenium import webdriver
from selenium.webdriver.common.by import By
from selenium.webdriver.common.keys import Keys
import time

driver = webdriver.Chrome(executable_path='path/to/chromedriver')
driver.get("https://www.example.com")

# Step 1: Log in
driver.find_element(By.ID, "username").send_keys("test_user")
driver.find_element(By.ID,
"password").send_keys("test_password")
driver.find_element(By.ID,
"password").send_keys(Keys.RETURN)
time.sleep(2)

# Step 2: Add item to cart
driver.find_element(By.ID, "add-to-cart-button").click()
time.sleep(1)

# Step 3: Go to checkout
driver.find_element(By.ID, "checkout-button").click()
```

```
time.sleep(2)


# Step 4: Verify checkout page and complete purchase
assert "checkout" in driver.current_url, "Failed to navigate to
checkout page."
driver.find_element(By.ID, "confirm-button").click()


print("End-to-end checkout test passed.")
driver.quit()
```

This script simulates an end-to-end test of the checkout process. It verifies that each step (login, adding items to the cart, navigating to checkout) is functioning correctly.

In this chapter, you learned how to use Selenium for browser automation, including controlling the browser, automating repetitive tasks like form filling and data extraction, and performing automated web tests to verify functionality. These techniques are powerful for tasks that involve repetitive web interactions and for validating web application behavior automatically. In the next chapter, we'll dive into automating social media tasks, expanding on browser automation to streamline interactions with social media platforms.

CHAPTER 11: AUTOMATING SOCIAL MEDIA TASKS

Social media is a key component of modern digital marketing, and automation can save significant time and resources for businesses, brands, and individuals managing multiple social accounts. By automating tasks such as posting, scheduling, and data collection, you can ensure consistent engagement, optimize your posting schedule, and gather insights for performance analysis. In this chapter, we'll explore how to post content to social media platforms via APIs, schedule posts, and automate social media data collection and analytics.

11.1 Posting to Social Media Platforms via APIs

Most major social media platforms provide APIs that allow programmatic access to features such as posting content, retrieving followers, and engaging with users. The most commonly automated platforms include Twitter, Facebook, and Instagram, each with its API.

Getting Started with APIs and Authentication

Each social media API requires an authentication process, usually involving API keys or OAuth tokens. To start, you'll need to create an account on the platform's developer site and register an application to get your API credentials. Below are links to developer portals for major platforms:

- **Twitter**: Twitter Developer Platform
- **Facebook and Instagram**: Meta for Developers
- **LinkedIn**: LinkedIn Developer Network

Installation for Common API Libraries:

- **Twitter**: tweepy

bash

pip install tweepy

Posting Content on Twitter using the Tweepy Library

The Twitter API is a popular choice for automating tweets, retweets, and engagement. Here's an example of using Tweepy to post a tweet.

Example Recipe: Posting a Tweet

python

```
import tweepy

# API credentials (replace with your own keys)
consumer_key = "your_consumer_key"
consumer_secret = "your_consumer_secret"
access_token = "your_access_token"
access_token_secret = "your_access_token_secret"

# Authenticate with Twitter API
auth = tweepy.OAuthHandler(consumer_key, consumer_secret)
auth.set_access_token(access_token, access_token_secret)
api = tweepy.API(auth)

# Post a tweet
tweet_content = "Automated tweet using Tweepy and Python!"
api.update_status(tweet_content)
```

```
print("Tweet posted successfully.")
```

This script authenticates with the Twitter API and posts a tweet. Replace the credentials with your own, and adjust tweet_content to customize the message.

Posting on Instagram using the Facebook Graph API

Instagram's API requires setting up a Facebook App and using the Facebook Graph API, which handles authentication for both Facebook and Instagram.

Example Recipe: Posting an Image to Instagram

This example posts an image to Instagram, assuming the Instagram account is connected to a Facebook page.

1. Authenticate using the Facebook Graph API to get an access token.
2. Use the media_publish endpoint to post the image.

python

```python
import requests

# API credentials
access_token = "your_access_token"
instagram_account_id = "your_instagram_account_id"
image_url = "https://your-image-url.jpg"
```

```python
caption = "Automated post using the Instagram Graph API!"

# Prepare the API request
url = f"https://graph.facebook.com/v14.0/{instagram_account_id}/media"
params = {
    "image_url": image_url,
    "caption": caption,
    "access_token": access_token
}
response = requests.post(url, params=params)
media_id = response.json()["id"]

# Publish the image to Instagram
publish_url = f"https://graph.facebook.com/v14.0/{instagram_account_id}/media_publish"
publish_params = {
    "creation_id": media_id,
    "access_token": access_token
}
publish_response = requests.post(publish_url, params=publish_params)
```

print("Instagram post published successfully.")

This script first creates media with the image and caption, then publishes it. Make sure to replace the access_token, instagram_account_id, and image_url with your information.

11.2 Scheduling Social Media Posts

Scheduling social media posts is a useful feature for maintaining a regular posting schedule. This can be achieved by setting up Python scripts to post at specific times using the schedule library, or by using third-party platforms with Python integrations.

Scheduling Posts with the schedule Library

Using the schedule library, you can automate post timing. Here's an example of scheduling a tweet to go out every Monday at 9:00 AM.

Example Recipe: Scheduling Weekly Tweets

python

```
import schedule
import time
import tweepy

# Twitter API setup as in previous example
auth = tweepy.OAuthHandler(consumer_key, consumer_secret)
auth.set_access_token(access_token, access_token_secret)
```

```
api = tweepy.API(auth)

def post_weekly_tweet():
    tweet_content = "Weekly scheduled tweet using Python!"
    api.update_status(tweet_content)
    print("Weekly tweet posted.")

# Schedule the tweet every Monday at 9:00 AM
schedule.every().monday.at("09:00").do(post_weekly_tweet)

while True:
    schedule.run_pending()
    time.sleep(1)
```

This script uses schedule to trigger a tweet every Monday at 9:00 AM, simulating a basic scheduling tool.

Using Buffer API for Multi-Platform Scheduling

Buffer provides an API to manage and schedule posts across multiple social media platforms, like Twitter, Facebook, and LinkedIn. Using Buffer can simplify cross-platform scheduling.

Example Recipe: Scheduling a Post via Buffer

1. Create a Buffer account and get an access token.
2. Use the Buffer API to schedule a post.

python

```python
import requests

# Buffer API credentials
access_token = "your_buffer_access_token"
profile_ids = ["your_profile_id"]   # Add profile IDs for each platform (e.g., Twitter, Facebook)

url = "https://api.bufferapp.com/1/updates/create.json"
data = {
    "text": "Scheduled post using Buffer API!",
    "profile_ids[]": profile_ids,
    "scheduled_at": "2023-12-01T09:00:00Z", # UTC format
    "access_token": access_token
}

response = requests.post(url, data=data)
print("Scheduled post response:", response.json())
```

This code schedules a post to be published via Buffer. You can set up different profile_ids for different social media accounts, simplifying multi-platform scheduling.

11.3 Automating Social Media Data Collection and Analytics

Tracking performance metrics, engagement, and audience growth is crucial for social media strategy. APIs from Twitter, Facebook, and Instagram allow access to follower counts, likes, shares, and other metrics, which you can then automate and analyze.

Collecting Twitter Metrics

Twitter's API enables you to gather data on tweet performance, followers, and engagement. Here's an example of collecting data on recent tweets.

Example Recipe: Collecting Twitter Engagement Metrics

This script retrieves the latest tweets and their engagement metrics (likes, retweets) for a specified user.

python

```python
import tweepy

# Twitter API setup as in previous examples
auth = tweepy.OAuthHandler(consumer_key, consumer_secret)
auth.set_access_token(access_token, access_token_secret)
api = tweepy.API(auth)

# Fetch recent tweets and display engagement metrics
tweets = api.user_timeline(screen_name="your_username", count=5)

for tweet in tweets:
```

```
print(f"Tweet: {tweet.text}")
```

```
print(f"Likes:        {tweet.favorite_count},        Retweets: {tweet.retweet_count}")
```

This script retrieves the five latest tweets for a specified user and prints each tweet's engagement metrics.

Gathering Instagram Insights with the Graph API

Instagram's Graph API provides access to engagement metrics for business accounts, including follower count, post likes, and reach.

Example Recipe: Collecting Instagram Analytics

1. Use the Facebook Graph API to gather insights.
2. Specify the metric parameters for engagement data.

python

```
import requests
```

```
# Access token and Instagram business account ID
access_token = "your_access_token"
instagram_account_id = "your_instagram_account_id"
```

```
# Define metrics to retrieve
metrics = "impressions,reach,engagement,followers_count"
```

```
url                                                    =
f"https://graph.facebook.com/v14.0/{instagram_account_id}/insig
hts?metric={metrics}&access_token={access_token}"

response = requests.get(url)
data = response.json()

# Display metrics
for insight in data["data"]:
    print(f"{insight['title']}: {insight['values'][0]['value']}")
```

This script fetches Instagram engagement metrics like impressions, reach, engagement, and followers count for a specified business account.

Automating Report Generation for Social Media Metrics

Once you've collected social media data, you can automate report generation for a quick overview of social media performance.

Example Recipe: Generating a Weekly Social Media Report

This script collects metrics from multiple social media platforms and exports the data to a CSV report.

python

```
import tweepy
import requests
```

```python
import pandas as pd
from datetime import datetime

# Twitter setup
twitter_api = tweepy.API(auth)

# Instagram setup
instagram_access_token = "your_instagram_access_token"
instagram_account_id = "your_instagram_account_id"
instagram_metrics_url                                    =
f"https://graph.facebook.com/v14.0/{instagram_account_id}/insig
hts?metric=impressions,reach,engagement&access_token={instagr
am_access_token}"

# Collect Twitter data
tweets = twitter_api.user_timeline(screen_name="your_username",
count=5)
twitter_data = [{"Platform": "Twitter", "Text": tweet.text, "Likes":
tweet.favorite_count, "Retweets": tweet.retweet_count} for tweet
in tweets]

# Collect Instagram data
instagram_data                                           =
requests.get(instagram_metrics_url).json()["data"]
```

```python
instagram_metrics = [{"Platform": "Instagram", metric["title"]:
metric["values"][0]["value"]} for metric in instagram_data]

# Combine data
report_data = twitter_data + instagram_metrics
df = pd.DataFrame(report_data)

# Export report to CSV
df.to_csv(f"social_media_report_{datetime.now().strftime('%Y-
%m-%d')}.csv", index=False)
print("Weekly social media report generated.")
```

This script pulls recent metrics from Twitter and Instagram and saves them into a single CSV report for easy review.

In this chapter, you learned how to automate social media tasks, including posting via APIs, scheduling posts with libraries like schedule and Buffer, and collecting social media data for analytics. These techniques can save time, ensure consistent engagement, and provide valuable insights for optimizing social media strategy. Next, we'll look at system monitoring and alerts, helping you maintain a proactive approach to managing your digital environment.

CHAPTER 12: INTERACTING WITH OPERATING SYSTEMS

Python's built-in libraries allow it to interact directly with operating systems, making it highly effective for automating system-level tasks, performing system monitoring, and managing files across platforms. In this chapter, we'll explore how to automate OS commands, monitor system performance (CPU and memory usage), and perform file management tasks compatible with Windows, Mac, and Linux.

12.1 Automating OS Commands with Python

Python's os and subprocess libraries allow you to interact with the operating system to execute commands, manage processes, and automate tasks such as managing files, users, and services.

Running OS Commands with os.system()

The os.system() function executes commands directly in the system shell, allowing you to automate command-line tasks.

Example Recipe: Automating Directory Creation and File Listing

This script creates a directory and lists files within it using os.system() commands.

python

```
import os

# Create a new directory
os.system("mkdir automated_directory")

# List files in the new directory
os.system("ls -l automated_directory")  # Use "dir" on Windows
```

On Linux/macOS, ls lists files, while on Windows, you'd use dir.

Running Commands with subprocess.run()

The subprocess library provides more flexibility and control over system commands, allowing you to capture output, handle errors, and chain commands.

Example Recipe: Running a System Update and Capturing Output

This example shows how to use subprocess.run() to run system update commands and capture output.

python

```
import subprocess

# Run a system update (Linux/macOS example)
result = subprocess.run(["sudo", "apt-get", "update"],
capture_output=True, text=True)

# Print output and check for errors
print("Output:", result.stdout)
print("Errors:", result.stderr)
```

This script runs a system update and prints the command's output and any error messages. On Windows, you could run equivalent commands such as package updates using choco upgrade if Chocolatey is installed.

12.2 Using Python for System Monitoring (CPU, Memory)

Python can monitor CPU and memory usage, making it suitable for automated performance monitoring and resource management. The psutil library provides an easy way to access system information.

Installing psutil

Install psutil for system monitoring:

bash

pip install psutil

Monitoring CPU and Memory Usage

psutil can retrieve information on CPU utilization, memory usage, and other system metrics.

Example Recipe: Monitoring CPU and Memory Usage

This script retrieves and displays real-time CPU and memory usage.

python

```python
import psutil
import time

# Monitor CPU and memory usage
while True:
    cpu_percent = psutil.cpu_percent(interval=1)
    memory_info = psutil.virtual_memory()

    print(f"CPU Usage: {cpu_percent}%")
    print(f"Memory Usage: {memory_info.percent}%")

    time.sleep(5)  # Update every 5 seconds
```

This script continuously monitors and displays the system's CPU and memory usage every five seconds, providing a live update.

Setting Alerts for High Usage

You can set alerts to notify you if CPU or memory usage exceeds a threshold, which is helpful for managing resource-heavy applications.

Example Recipe: Alerting for High CPU or Memory Usage

This script checks CPU and memory usage and prints an alert if usage exceeds a specified threshold.

python

```python
import psutil
import time

CPU_THRESHOLD = 80  # percent
MEMORY_THRESHOLD = 80  # percent

while True:
    cpu_percent = psutil.cpu_percent(interval=1)
    memory_percent = psutil.virtual_memory().percent

    if cpu_percent > CPU_THRESHOLD:
        print(f"ALERT:    High    CPU    usage    detected    -
{cpu_percent}%")

    if memory_percent > MEMORY_THRESHOLD:
        print(f"ALERT:    High    Memory    usage    detected    -
{memory_percent}%")

    time.sleep(5)
```

This code sends alerts if CPU or memory usage exceeds 80%, helping you monitor potential performance issues in real time.

12.3 File Management Automation on Multiple Platforms (Windows, Mac, Linux)

Python's os and shutil libraries provide cross-platform functionality for file and directory management. This section covers creating, moving, and deleting files and directories with scripts that work on Windows, Mac, and Linux.

Creating and Organizing Files and Folders

Automating file and folder creation is useful for setting up project structures, organizing files, and preparing environments.

Example Recipe: Creating a Project Directory Structure

This script creates a structured set of directories for a new project, organizing folders for documents, data, and scripts.

python

```
import os

# Define the directory structure
project_name = "new_project"
folders = ["documents", "data", "scripts"]

# Create the project directory and subdirectories
os.makedirs(project_name, exist_ok=True)
for folder in folders:
    os.makedirs(os.path.join(project_name, folder), exist_ok=True)

print(f"Project structure created for '{project_name}'.")
```

This script uses os.makedirs() to create the main project directory along with subdirectories, making it easy to set up a consistent project structure.

Moving and Copying Files

Python's shutil library provides tools to copy, move, and delete files, making it easy to automate file management tasks.

Example Recipe: Moving and Copying Files Between Directories

This example copies a file from one directory to another and then moves it to a new location.

python

```
import shutil

# Copy a file
shutil.copy("source_directory/file.txt",
"destination_directory/file.txt")

# Move the file to a different directory
shutil.move("destination_directory/file.txt",
"final_directory/file.txt")

print("File copied and moved successfully.")
```

This script copies a file from one directory to another and then moves it, helping automate tasks such as organizing downloaded files or archiving.

Deleting Files and Directories

Automating deletion is useful for clearing temporary files, cleaning up directories, or removing outdated backups.

Example Recipe: Deleting Old Files Based on Age

This script deletes files older than a specified number of days in a directory.

python

```
import os
import time

directory = "temp_files"
days_to_keep = 7
now = time.time()

# Delete files older than specified days
for filename in os.listdir(directory):
    file_path = os.path.join(directory, filename)
    if os.path.isfile(file_path):
        file_age = now - os.path.getmtime(file_path)
        if file_age > days_to_keep * 86400:
            os.remove(file_path)
            print(f"Deleted {filename} - Age: {file_age / 86400:.1f}
days")
```

This script calculates each file's age in the temp_files directory and deletes those older than seven days, making it easy to automate cleanup tasks.

Cross-Platform File Management Tips

Python's os.path library handles path differences between Windows, Mac, and Linux. Here's a list of best practices for cross-platform compatibility:

1. **Path Separation**: Use os.path.join() to construct file paths, which ensures compatibility across platforms.

    python

    path = os.path.join("directory", "subdirectory", "file.txt")

2. **File Permissions**: On Linux/macOS, you may need to set permissions for certain files. Use os.chmod() to manage permissions.
3. **Environment Variables**: Access environment variables with os.environ for OS-independent configuration management.

In this chapter, you learned how to interact with operating systems using Python, automate OS commands, monitor CPU and memory performance, and manage files and directories across multiple platforms. These skills provide you with the tools needed to handle system-level tasks, automate system monitoring, and ensure efficient file organization in any environment. In the next chapter, we'll explore working with spreadsheets for data entry and reporting automation, leveraging Python's capabilities for handling Excel files.

CHAPTER 13: WORKING WITH EXCEL AND SPREADSHEETS

Excel is a cornerstone for data storage and analysis in many industries. Automating data entry and manipulation in Excel can significantly enhance productivity, especially for tasks involving repetitive data entry, reporting, and formatting. In this chapter, we'll explore how to automate data entry, formatting, and manipulation in Excel using Python's openpyxl and pandas libraries. We'll also cover how to build reusable scripts to streamline spreadsheet automation.

13.1 Automating Data Entry and Formatting in Excel

Automating data entry in Excel allows for efficient reporting, data processing, and even dynamic spreadsheet updates. Using openpyxl, you can automate tasks such as inserting data into cells, applying formatting, and adding formulas.

Setting Up openpyxl and pandas

Install openpyxl and pandas if you haven't already:

bash

pip install openpyxl pandas

Writing Data to Excel with openpyxl

The openpyxl library allows you to create Excel files, write data into cells, and apply basic formatting. This example shows how to create a new Excel file and enter data into specific cells.

Example Recipe: Creating an Excel Report with Basic Data Entry

python

```python
from openpyxl import Workbook

# Create a new workbook and select the active sheet
wb = Workbook()
ws = wb.active
ws.title = "Monthly Sales Report"

# Enter headers
ws["A1"] = "Date"
ws["B1"] = "Product"
ws["C1"] = "Quantity"
ws["D1"] = "Revenue"

# Enter data
data = [
    ["2023-01-01", "Product A", 10, 100],
    ["2023-01-02", "Product B", 5, 50],
    ["2023-01-03", "Product C", 8, 80],
```

```
]
```

```python
for row in data:
    ws.append(row)
```

```python
# Save the file
wb.save("monthly_sales_report.xlsx")
print("Excel report created.")
```

This script creates a new Excel file named monthly_sales_report.xlsx with headers and data entries. ws.append(row) makes it easy to add rows to the worksheet.

Formatting Cells in Excel

With openpyxl, you can apply cell formatting to improve the readability of your reports. Formatting includes changing font style, color, alignment, and more.

Example Recipe: Formatting Cells in Excel

python

```python
from openpyxl.styles import Font, Alignment, PatternFill
```

```python
# Load workbook and select the sheet
wb = Workbook()
ws = wb.active
ws.title = "Formatted Report"
```

```python
# Add headers
headers = ["Date", "Product", "Quantity", "Revenue"]
ws.append(headers)

# Apply header formatting
for cell in ws[1]:
    cell.font = Font(bold=True, color="FFFFFF")
    cell.fill = PatternFill(start_color="4F81BD",
end_color="4F81BD", fill_type="solid")
    cell.alignment = Alignment(horizontal="center")

# Add sample data
data = [
    ["2023-01-01", "Product A", 10, 100],
    ["2023-01-02", "Product B", 5, 50],
]
for row in data:
    ws.append(row)

# Save the file
wb.save("formatted_report.xlsx")
print("Formatted Excel report created.")
```

This code applies bold text and background color to the headers, improving the visual appeal of the report. Each cell in the header row is styled individually for greater flexibility.

13.2 Using openpyxl and pandas for Spreadsheet Manipulation

pandas offers robust data manipulation tools that, when combined with openpyxl, can streamline the creation and updating of complex spreadsheets. This section covers how to read and write Excel files using pandas, making it easy to automate data processing and reporting tasks.

Reading Excel Files with pandas

pandas can read Excel files directly into DataFrames, which simplifies analysis and manipulation.

Example Recipe: Reading an Excel File into a DataFrame

python

```
import pandas as pd

# Load the Excel file
df = pd.read_excel("sales_data.xlsx")

# Display the first few rows
print(df.head())
```

This script reads an Excel file into a DataFrame, making it easy to view, manipulate, and analyze data.

Writing Data to Excel with pandas

You can also write DataFrames to Excel files, which is useful for exporting cleaned or analyzed data back into a spreadsheet format.

Example Recipe: Writing a DataFrame to Excel

python

```
# Data to write
data = {
    "Date": ["2023-01-01", "2023-01-02", "2023-01-03"],
    "Product": ["Product A", "Product B", "Product C"],
    "Quantity": [10, 5, 8],
    "Revenue": [100, 50, 80]
}
df = pd.DataFrame(data)

# Write to Excel
df.to_excel("sales_report.xlsx", index=False)
print("Data written to Excel.")
```

This script writes a DataFrame to an Excel file without including the index column, creating a clean, tabular report.

Combining pandas and openpyxl for Data Manipulation and Formatting

Using pandas to manipulate data and openpyxl to format it allows you to handle more complex reporting requirements.

Example Recipe: Analyzing and Formatting Data

This example reads sales data, calculates total revenue, and applies formatting before saving to a new Excel file.

python

```python
from openpyxl import load_workbook
import pandas as pd

# Load sales data
df = pd.read_excel("raw_sales_data.xlsx")

# Add a total revenue column
df["Total Revenue"] = df["Quantity"] * df["Price"]

# Write updated data to Excel
df.to_excel("processed_sales_report.xlsx", index=False)

# Load workbook and apply formatting
wb = load_workbook("processed_sales_report.xlsx")
ws = wb.active
```

```
# Apply bold formatting to header row
for cell in ws[1]:
    cell.font = Font(bold=True)
```

```
wb.save("processed_sales_report.xlsx")
print("Processed and formatted Excel report saved.")
```

This script calculates total revenue for each row and formats the header row. By using both pandas and openpyxl, you can achieve efficient data manipulation and presentable formatting in one workflow.

13.3 Building Reusable Scripts for Spreadsheet Automation

Reusable scripts allow you to define functions for repetitive spreadsheet tasks, such as applying consistent formatting, calculating summary statistics, and organizing data. This section covers building functions that make it easy to reuse code for similar tasks across multiple projects.

Creating a Function for Data Entry and Formatting

Example Recipe: Function to Write Data and Apply Formatting

This function writes data to an Excel file, applies header formatting, and saves the file.

python

```python
from openpyxl import Workbook
from openpyxl.styles import Font

def create_excel_report(data, filename="report.xlsx"):
    wb = Workbook()
    ws = wb.active

    # Write headers and apply formatting
    headers = data[0].keys()
    ws.append(list(headers))
    for cell in ws[1]:
        cell.font = Font(bold=True)

    # Write data
    for row in data:
        ws.append(list(row.values()))

    # Save file
    wb.save(filename)
    print(f"Report saved as {filename}")

# Sample data
data = [
    {"Date": "2023-01-01", "Product": "Product A", "Quantity": 10,
"Revenue": 100},
```

```
{"Date": "2023-01-02", "Product": "Product B", "Quantity": 5,
"Revenue": 50},
]
```

create_excel_report(data, filename="custom_report.xlsx")
This function takes data as a list of dictionaries and writes it to an Excel file with formatted headers, making it easy to reuse for similar reporting tasks.

Creating a Function to Merge Multiple Sheets into a Single Workbook

If you need to consolidate data from multiple sources, this function creates a workbook with multiple sheets.

Example Recipe: Function to Merge Sheets from Different DataFrames

python

```python
import pandas as pd
from openpyxl import Workbook


def             merge_sheets(dataframes,             sheet_names,
filename="merged_workbook.xlsx"):
    wb = Workbook()
    for df, sheet_name in zip(dataframes, sheet_names):
        ws = wb.create_sheet(title=sheet_name)
```

```
    for row in pd.DataFrame(df).itertuples(index=False):
        ws.append(row)
    wb.save(filename)
    print(f"Workbook saved as {filename}")


# Sample data
df1 = pd.DataFrame({"A": [1, 2], "B": [3, 4]})
df2 = pd.DataFrame({"X": [5, 6], "Y": [7, 8]})


merge_sheets([df1,        df2],        ["Sheet1",        "Sheet2"],
"combined_report.xlsx")
```

This function creates a workbook with multiple sheets from separate DataFrames, providing a straightforward way to combine and organize data across multiple sources.

Building a Function for Monthly Report Generation

Automating monthly reports can save time on recurring tasks. This function generates monthly reports by processing data, calculating totals, and applying formatting.

Example Recipe: Monthly Report Generation

python

```
def              generate_monthly_report(data,              month,
filename="monthly_report.xlsx"):
    df = pd.DataFrame(data)
```

```python
df["Total Revenue"] = df["Quantity"] * df["Price"]
monthly_total = df["Total Revenue"].sum()


# Write data to Excel
with pd.ExcelWriter(filename) as writer:
    df.to_excel(writer, sheet_name=month, index=False)
    summary      =      pd.DataFrame({"Total      Revenue":
[monthly_total]})
    summary.to_excel(writer, sheet_name="Summary")


    print(f"{month} report saved as {filename}")

# Sample data for January
data = [
    {"Date": "2023-01-01", "Product": "Product A", "Quantity": 10,
"Price": 10},
    {"Date": "2023-01-02", "Product": "Product B", "Quantity": 5,
"Price": 15},
]


generate_monthly_report(data, "January", "january_report.xlsx")
```

This function generates a monthly report with data and a summary sheet, providing a template for creating recurring reports with minimal setup.

In this chapter, you learned how to automate data entry, formatting, and manipulation in Excel using Python's openpyxl and pandas libraries. By building reusable functions, you can streamline recurring tasks, ensuring consistency across reports and saving time. The next chapter will explore text-based data processing and how to automate email content creation, focusing on NLP and templating tools to manage large volumes of text data efficiently.

CHAPTER 14: AUTOMATING TASK TRACKING AND TO-DO LISTS

Task tracking and to-do list management are essential for staying organized and productive, especially when juggling multiple projects or deadlines. Automating task management using Python can help streamline daily routines, provide timely reminders, and maintain up-to-date task lists. This chapter explores how to create and update task lists automatically, integrate Python with popular productivity tools like Google Tasks and Trello, and automate daily task reminders.

14.1 Creating and Updating Task Lists Automatically

Using Python, you can create, update, and manage task lists in a format that's accessible across devices. This section covers creating a basic to-do list in Python and automating updates to it.

Setting Up a Simple To-Do List System

A basic to-do list can be created and managed using Python's standard libraries, such as csv for structured storage or json for more complex data needs.

Example Recipe: Creating a Simple To-Do List in CSV

This script creates a basic to-do list stored in a CSV file and updates it as tasks are added or marked complete.

python

```python
import csv

# Define CSV file for storing tasks
csv_file = "tasks.csv"

# Function to add a task
def add_task(task, status="Pending"):
    with open(csv_file, "a", newline="") as file:
        writer = csv.writer(file)
        writer.writerow([task, status])
    print(f"Task '{task}' added.")

# Function to display tasks
def display_tasks():
    with open(csv_file, "r") as file:
        reader = csv.reader(file)
        print("To-Do List:")
        for row in reader:
            print(f"Task: {row[0]}, Status: {row[1]}")

# Function to mark task as complete
def complete_task(task_name):
    tasks = []
```

```
with open(csv_file, "r") as file:
    reader = csv.reader(file)
    for row in reader:
        if row[0] == task_name:
            row[1] = "Complete"
        tasks.append(row)
with open(csv_file, "w", newline="") as file:
    writer = csv.writer(file)
    writer.writerows(tasks)
print(f"Task '{task_name}' marked as complete.")


# Example usage
add_task("Finish monthly report")
add_task("Prepare meeting agenda")
display_tasks()
complete_task("Finish monthly report")
display_tasks()
```

This script allows you to add tasks, display them, and mark them as complete. The tasks are stored in tasks.csv, which can be opened in any spreadsheet application for easy viewing.

14.2 Integrating Python with Productivity Tools (Google Tasks, Trello)

Many productivity tools, such as Google Tasks and Trello, offer APIs that allow Python to interact with them. These integrations enable you to automate task creation, update statuses, and sync data across platforms.

Google Tasks API Integration

Google Tasks is a part of Google Workspace and provides an API for managing to-do lists and tasks. To use the Google Tasks API, you need to set up a project on the Google Cloud Console, enable the Tasks API, and obtain OAuth credentials.

Example Recipe: Adding Tasks to Google Tasks with Python

1. First, install the Google API client library:

   bash

   pip install --upgrade google-auth google-auth-oauthlib google-auth-httplib2 google-api-python-client

2. Set up authentication using OAuth 2.0 credentials.
3. Use the following code to add a task to Google Tasks.

python

from google.oauth2 import service_account
from googleapiclient.discovery import build

# Authentication and setup
SCOPES = ['https://www.googleapis.com/auth/tasks']

```python
credentials                                              =
service_account.Credentials.from_service_account_file('path/to/cr
edentials.json', scopes=SCOPES)
service = build('tasks', 'v1', credentials=credentials)


# Function to add a task
def add_google_task(task_title):
    task = {"title": task_title}
    result         =        service.tasks().insert(tasklist="@default",
body=task).execute()
    print(f"Added task: {result['title']}")


# Example usage
add_google_task("Complete Python automation script")
```

This script authenticates with Google Tasks using service account credentials, adds a task to the default task list, and confirms the addition. Adjust the authentication method if using personal credentials instead of a service account.

Trello API Integration

Trello is a popular task management and collaboration tool that provides an API for automating board and task management. To use the Trello API, you need an API key and token from the Trello Developer Portal.

Example Recipe: Adding a Card to a Trello Board

1. Install requests if not already installed:

   bash

   pip install requests

2. Use the following code to add a new card to a Trello board.

python

import requests

# Trello API credentials
api_key = "your_api_key"
token = "your_api_token"
board_id = "your_board_id"
list_id = "your_list_id" # List within the board where the task will be added

# Function to add a card to Trello
def add_trello_card(card_name, card_desc):
    url = f"https://api.trello.com/1/cards"
    query = {
        'key': api_key,
        'token': token,
        'idList': list_id,

```
        'name': card_name,
        'desc': card_desc
    }
    response = requests.post(url, params=query)
    if response.status_code == 200:
        print(f"Card '{card_name}' added to Trello.")
    else:
        print("Failed to add card to Trello:", response.status_code)


# Example usage
add_trello_card("Research Python Trello integration", "Explore Trello API for automation.")
```

This code adds a card to a specified list on a Trello board, helping you manage tasks directly in Trello using Python.

14.3 Automating Daily Task Reminders

Automating daily reminders ensures you stay on top of tasks without needing to manually check to-do lists. Python's schedule library or built-in task scheduling tools can be used to send daily reminders.

Sending Task Reminders via Email

You can set up an automated email reminder system that sends you a summary of tasks for the day.

Example Recipe: Daily Email Reminder for Tasks

This example gathers tasks from a CSV file and sends an email reminder with the list of pending tasks.

1. Install smtplib and email for sending emails:

   python

   import smtplib
   from email.message import EmailMessage
   import csv
   import schedule
   import time

2. Define a function to send an email with the day's tasks.

python

```
# Define the CSV file for tasks
csv_file = "tasks.csv"

# Function to get tasks from CSV
def get_pending_tasks():
    tasks = []
    with open(csv_file, "r") as file:
        reader = csv.reader(file)
        for row in reader:
            if row[1] == "Pending":
```

```python
        tasks.append(row[0])
    return tasks


# Function to send daily email reminder
def send_email_reminder():
    tasks = get_pending_tasks()
    if not tasks:
        print("No pending tasks for today.")
        return


    # Email details
    sender = "your_email@example.com"
    recipient = "recipient_email@example.com"
    subject = "Daily Task Reminder"
    body = "Here are your pending tasks for today:\n\n" + "\n".join(tasks)


    # Set up email
    msg = EmailMessage()
    msg["From"] = sender
    msg["To"] = recipient
    msg["Subject"] = subject
    msg.set_content(body)


    # Send email
```

```
with smtplib.SMTP_SSL("smtp.gmail.com", 465) as smtp:
    smtp.login(sender, "your_password")
    smtp.send_message(msg)


    print("Daily task reminder sent.")

# Schedule daily email at 8:00 AM
schedule.every().day.at("08:00").do(send_email_reminder)


# Keep script running to execute scheduled tasks
while True:
    schedule.run_pending()
    time.sleep(60)
```

This script sends an email with the list of pending tasks each day at 8:00 AM. Replace the email credentials with your own, and configure csv_file to match your task file location.

Setting Up Notifications with Desktop Alerts

If email reminders are not necessary, you can use Python to create desktop notifications for tasks using the plyer library.

1. Install plyer:

   bash

   pip install plyer

2. Use plyer.notification to create a desktop alert.

Example Recipe: Desktop Task Reminder

python

```python
from plyer import notification
import schedule
import time
import csv

# Load pending tasks
def get_tasks():
    tasks = []
    with open("tasks.csv", "r") as file:
        reader = csv.reader(file)
        for row in reader:
            if row[1] == "Pending":
                tasks.append(row[0])
    return tasks

# Function for desktop notification
def task_notification():
    tasks = get_tasks()
    if tasks:
        notification.notify(
```

```
        title="Daily Task Reminder",
        message="Pending tasks:\n" + "\n".join(tasks),
        timeout=10
    )
  else:
    print("No pending tasks.")


# Schedule daily reminder at 8:00 AM
schedule.every().day.at("08:00").do(task_notification)


while True:
  schedule.run_pending()
  time.sleep(60)
```

This script shows a desktop notification with a list of pending tasks every morning at 8:00 AM. You can customize the frequency and task list source as needed.

In this chapter, you learned how to automate task tracking and to-do list management. Using Python, you created a basic to-do list, integrated with productivity tools like Google Tasks and Trello, and set up automated daily reminders via email and desktop notifications. Automating task management can help you stay organized, avoid missed deadlines, and maintain focus on important tasks. In the next chapter, we'll dive into building command-line tools for efficient, script-based interactions with these automated workflows.

CHAPTER 15: BUILDING CHATBOTS FOR DAILY ASSISTANCE

Chatbots are increasingly popular for automating interactions and providing quick, accessible assistance across various domains. From customer support to personal reminders, chatbots offer practical, hands-free solutions. In this chapter, we'll introduce chatbot development, explore how to create a simple text-based chatbot, and learn how to automate responses for frequently asked questions (FAQs).

15.1 Introduction to Chatbot Development

A chatbot is an application designed to simulate conversation with human users, often for specific purposes like answering questions, assisting with tasks, or managing reminders. Chatbots can be developed using simple rule-based systems, where responses are triggered by keywords, or more advanced natural language processing (NLP) models.

Types of Chatbots

1. **Rule-Based Chatbots**: These chatbots follow predefined rules and respond based on specific keywords or patterns. They are suitable for simple tasks and FAQs.

2. **AI-Powered Chatbots**: These chatbots use machine learning and NLP to understand and generate responses.

They are more adaptable and can handle complex interactions but require training data.

Tools for Building Chatbots

1. **NLTK and SpaCy**: Libraries for natural language processing that help parse text, recognize keywords, and manage conversations.
2. **Dialogflow, Rasa, and BotPress**: Frameworks that provide NLP capabilities and interfaces for building and deploying chatbots.

For this chapter, we'll focus on creating a simple text-based chatbot using Python and basic NLP techniques.

15.2 Creating a Simple Text-Based Chatbot

A simple chatbot can respond to basic commands or keywords. This type of chatbot can be built using conditional statements or pattern matching with regular expressions, making it ideal for task reminders or quick Q&A functionality.

Setting Up a Basic Chatbot Framework

A rule-based chatbot can be built using Python's input() function for user input and conditional statements to generate responses.

Example Recipe: Creating a Basic Rule-Based Chatbot

This example demonstrates a basic chatbot that responds to a few specific questions or commands.

python

```python
def chatbot_response(user_input):
    user_input = user_input.lower()

    if "hello" in user_input:
        return "Hello! How can I assist you today?"
    elif "task" in user_input:
        return "Would you like to add, view, or complete a task?"
    elif "time" in user_input:
        from datetime import datetime
        return f"The current time is {datetime.now().strftime('%H:%M:%S')}."
    elif "bye" in user_input:
        return "Goodbye! Have a great day!"
    else:
        return "I'm sorry, I didn't understand that. Could you rephrase?"

# Running the chatbot in a loop
print("Welcome to your personal assistant chatbot! Type 'bye' to exit.")
while True:
```

```python
user_input = input("You: ")
if "bye" in user_input.lower():
    print("Chatbot:", chatbot_response(user_input))
    break
response = chatbot_response(user_input)
print("Chatbot:", response)
```

This chatbot can greet users, check the time, and interact with simple task-related requests. It processes each command by checking for keywords in the input text.

Enhancing the Chatbot with Pattern Matching

Using regular expressions, the chatbot can detect more specific phrases, providing flexibility in recognizing user intent.

Example Recipe: Chatbot with Pattern Matching for Tasks

This chatbot responds to task requests, such as "Add a task," "View tasks," or "Complete a task," using regular expressions for improved intent recognition.

python

```python
import re
```

```python
# Sample task list
tasks = []
```

```python
def chatbot_response(user_input):
    user_input = user_input.lower()

    # Greeting
    if re.search(r'\b(hi|hello)\b', user_input):
        return "Hello! I'm here to help you with your tasks."

    # Add a task
    elif re.search(r'add task', user_input):
        task = input("Chatbot: What task would you like to add? ")
        tasks.append(task)
        return f"Task '{task}' added successfully."

    # View tasks
    elif re.search(r'view tasks', user_input):
        if tasks:
            return "Here are your tasks:\n" + "\n".join(tasks)
        else:
            return "You have no tasks at the moment."

    # Complete a task
    elif re.search(r'complete task', user_input):
        task = input("Chatbot: Which task have you completed? ")
        if task in tasks:
            tasks.remove(task)
```

```
    return f"Task '{task}' marked as complete."
else:
    return f"Task '{task}' not found in your list."


# Default response
else:
    return "I'm not sure how to respond to that. Try saying 'add
task' or 'view tasks'."


# Running the chatbot
print("Welcome! Type 'bye' to exit.")
while True:
    user_input = input("You: ")
    if "bye" in user_input.lower():
        print("Chatbot: Goodbye! Have a productive day.")
        break
    response = chatbot_response(user_input)
    print("Chatbot:", response)
```

This chatbot manages a to-do list by adding, viewing, and completing tasks based on specific keywords. Regular expressions allow for flexible phrasing, making it more intuitive for users.

15.3 Automating Responses for Frequently Asked Questions (FAQs)

For businesses or personal use, a chatbot can answer FAQs based on predefined responses. This can save time by instantly addressing common queries without human intervention.

Creating a Dictionary-Based FAQ Bot

A dictionary-based FAQ bot maps specific questions to answers, allowing quick responses to known questions.

Example Recipe: FAQ Chatbot

This chatbot uses a dictionary to store common questions and answers, providing responses instantly.

python

```python
# Define FAQ responses
faq_responses = {
    "what is your name": "I'm your personal assistant bot!",
    "how can you help me": "I can assist with task management, reminders, and answering questions.",
    "what are your features": "I can add tasks, provide reminders, and answer FAQs."
}

def faq_chatbot_response(user_input):
    user_input = user_input.lower()
```

```
    response = faq_responses.get(user_input, "I'm sorry, I don't have
an answer for that.")
    return response


# Running the FAQ bot
print("Welcome to the FAQ bot! Ask a question or type 'bye' to
exit.")
while True:
    user_input = input("You: ")
    if "bye" in user_input.lower():
        print("Chatbot: Goodbye! Feel free to reach out anytime.")
        break
    response = faq_chatbot_response(user_input)
    print("Chatbot:", response)
```

This chatbot instantly responds to FAQs based on an internal dictionary of questions and answers, making it ideal for quick responses to routine queries.

Adding Fuzzy Matching for Flexible Responses

To make the FAQ bot more flexible, you can add fuzzy matching to recognize questions even if they're not phrased exactly as expected. The fuzzywuzzy library is helpful for this.

Example Recipe: FAQ Bot with Fuzzy Matching

1. Install fuzzywuzzy:

bash

```
pip install fuzzywuzzy[speedup]
```

2. Use the following code to implement fuzzy matching in the FAQ bot.

python

```
from fuzzywuzzy import fuzz
from fuzzywuzzy import process

# Define FAQ responses
faq_responses = {
    "what is your name": "I'm your personal assistant bot!",
    "how can you help me": "I can assist with task management, reminders, and answering questions.",
    "what are your features": "I can add tasks, provide reminders, and answer FAQs."
}

def faq_chatbot_fuzzy(user_input):
    # Find best match for user input
    question, score = process.extractOne(user_input, faq_responses.keys())
    if score > 75:  # Set a threshold for matching accuracy
```

```
    return faq_responses[question]
else:
    return "I'm sorry, I don't have an answer for that."


# Running the fuzzy-matching FAQ bot
print("Welcome to the FAQ bot! Ask a question or type 'bye' to exit.")
while True:
    user_input = input("You: ")
    if "bye" in user_input.lower():
        print("Chatbot: Goodbye! Feel free to ask anytime.")
        break
    response = faq_chatbot_fuzzy(user_input)
    print("Chatbot:", response)
```

This bot can recognize variations in phrasing, providing accurate responses even if the user's question isn't an exact match.

In this chapter, you learned how to build basic chatbots for daily assistance. We explored rule-based chatbots for task management, dictionary-based bots for answering FAQs, and fuzzy matching to make responses more flexible. Chatbots can be useful in personal productivity, customer support, and automated information delivery, providing quick, on-demand assistance. The next chapter will explore web scraping automation to gather information from the web and supplement chatbot knowledge bases with real-time data.

CHAPTER 16: AUTOMATING SYSTEM MONITORING AND ALERTS

Automating system monitoring and setting up alerts is essential for maintaining optimal performance, quickly identifying issues, and ensuring stability across applications, servers, or infrastructure. This chapter covers how to track server performance, monitor logs, set up automated alerts, and integrate monitoring scripts with communication channels such as Slack and email.

16.1 Tracking Server Performance and Logs

Tracking key performance metrics like CPU usage, memory consumption, disk space, and logs can help detect anomalies, prevent crashes, and improve troubleshooting efficiency. The psutil library in Python provides a convenient way to monitor system resources, while log files can be managed with Python's built-in libraries.

Monitoring CPU, Memory, and Disk Space

The psutil library can track system metrics in real time, enabling continuous monitoring of CPU, memory, and disk usage.

Example Recipe: Real-Time System Performance Monitoring

python

```python
import psutil
import time

def monitor_performance():
    while True:
        cpu_usage = psutil.cpu_percent(interval=1)
        memory_info = psutil.virtual_memory()
        disk_info = psutil.disk_usage('/')

        print(f"CPU Usage: {cpu_usage}%")
        print(f"Memory Usage: {memory_info.percent}%")
        print(f"Disk Usage: {disk_info.percent}%")

        time.sleep(5)  # Update every 5 seconds

monitor_performance()
```

This script provides a real-time update of CPU, memory, and disk usage every five seconds. Adjust the time.sleep() interval as needed for your monitoring frequency.

Monitoring System Logs

System logs contain valuable information about software, hardware, and system activity, which can be used to detect errors and unusual patterns. Python's logging library can monitor and process log files, making it easy to filter out errors or warnings.

Example Recipe: Filtering for Errors in Log Files

python

```
import re

def check_logs_for_errors(log_file):
    with open(log_file, "r") as file:
        for line in file:
            if re.search(r'ERROR|CRITICAL', line):
                print("Error detected:", line.strip())

# Example usage
check_logs_for_errors("system.log")
```

This script scans a log file for lines containing "ERROR" or "CRITICAL," helping you quickly identify problematic events in system logs.

16.2 Setting Up Automated Alerts and Notifications

Automated alerts allow you to respond quickly to critical issues, such as high resource usage or error spikes. By setting thresholds for CPU, memory, or disk space, you can trigger alerts when these limits are reached, ensuring that issues are addressed promptly.

Setting Thresholds for Alerts

Establish thresholds for CPU, memory, and disk usage to automate alerts. For example, you may want to receive an alert when CPU usage exceeds 80% or when disk space falls below 10% free.

Example Recipe: Triggering Alerts for High Resource Usage

python

```python
import psutil
import time


CPU_THRESHOLD = 80  # percent
MEMORY_THRESHOLD = 80  # percent
DISK_THRESHOLD = 90  # percent


def monitor_and_alert():
    while True:
        cpu_usage = psutil.cpu_percent(interval=1)
        memory_usage = psutil.virtual_memory().percent
        disk_usage = psutil.disk_usage('/').percent

        if cpu_usage > CPU_THRESHOLD:
```

```
        print(f"ALERT:    High    CPU    usage    detected    -
{cpu_usage}%")

    if memory_usage > MEMORY_THRESHOLD:
        print(f"ALERT:    High    Memory    usage    detected    -
{memory_usage}%")

    if disk_usage > DISK_THRESHOLD:
        print(f"ALERT:    High    Disk    usage    detected    -
{disk_usage}%")

    time.sleep(10)


monitor_and_alert()
```

This script monitors resource usage and prints an alert if any metric exceeds its threshold. You can modify the alert logic to include email or Slack notifications for remote monitoring.

16.3 Integrating Monitoring Scripts with Communication Channels (Slack, Email)

Automating alerts through communication channels like Slack and email ensures timely notifications when critical thresholds are breached, enabling you to act quickly. Here's how to set up alerts through both Slack and email.

Sending Alerts via Slack

To send messages to Slack, you can use Slack Webhooks. Set up a Slack Webhook URL by going to Slack API and creating a new webhook.

1. Install requests if it's not already installed:

   bash

   pip install requests

2. Use the Slack Webhook URL to send notifications.

Example Recipe: Sending Slack Alerts for High CPU Usage

python

```
import psutil
import time
import requests

# Slack Webhook URL
SLACK_WEBHOOK_URL                                    =
"https://hooks.slack.com/services/your/webhook/url"

CPU_THRESHOLD = 80

def send_slack_alert(message):
```

```
    data = {"text": message}
    response    =    requests.post(SLACK_WEBHOOK_URL,
json=data)
    if response.status_code == 200:
        print("Slack alert sent.")
    else:
        print("Failed to send Slack alert:", response.status_code)


def monitor_cpu():
    while True:
        cpu_usage = psutil.cpu_percent(interval=1)
        if cpu_usage > CPU_THRESHOLD:
            alert_message = f"ALERT: High CPU usage detected -
{cpu_usage}%"
            send_slack_alert(alert_message)
        time.sleep(10)


monitor_cpu()
```

This script monitors CPU usage and sends an alert to Slack if it exceeds 80%. Adjust the SLACK_WEBHOOK_URL with your own URL.

Sending Alerts via Email

You can automate email alerts using Python's smtplib library to notify you when resource usage is high or errors are detected in logs.

Example Recipe: Sending Email Alerts for High Memory Usage

1. Set up SMTP email settings (e.g., for Gmail, enable SMTP and create an app-specific password if necessary).
2. Define a function to send an email alert.

python

```python
import smtplib
from email.message import EmailMessage
import psutil
import time


# Email configuration
EMAIL_ADDRESS = "your_email@example.com"
EMAIL_PASSWORD = "your_email_password"
TO_ADDRESS = "recipient_email@example.com"
MEMORY_THRESHOLD = 80


def send_email_alert(subject, body):
    msg = EmailMessage()
    msg["From"] = EMAIL_ADDRESS
    msg["To"] = TO_ADDRESS
    msg["Subject"] = subject
    msg.set_content(body)
```

```python
    with smtplib.SMTP_SSL("smtp.gmail.com", 465) as smtp:
        smtp.login(EMAIL_ADDRESS, EMAIL_PASSWORD)
        smtp.send_message(msg)
        print("Email alert sent.")


def monitor_memory():
    while True:
        memory_usage = psutil.virtual_memory().percent
        if memory_usage > MEMORY_THRESHOLD:
            alert_message = f"ALERT: High Memory usage detected -
{memory_usage}%"
            send_email_alert("High      Memory      Usage      Alert",
alert_message)
        time.sleep(10)


monitor_memory()
```

This script monitors memory usage and sends an email alert if it exceeds the threshold. Customize EMAIL_ADDRESS, EMAIL_PASSWORD, and TO_ADDRESS with your credentials.

Combining Slack and Email Alerts for Comprehensive Monitoring

For enhanced monitoring, you can combine both Slack and email alerts, sending notifications to multiple channels for redundancy.

Example Recipe: Combined Slack and Email Alert System

```python
python

def combined_alert(message):
    send_slack_alert(message)
    send_email_alert("System Alert", message)

def monitor_system():
    while True:
        cpu_usage = psutil.cpu_percent(interval=1)
        memory_usage = psutil.virtual_memory().percent

        if cpu_usage > CPU_THRESHOLD:
            alert_message = f"High CPU usage detected - {cpu_usage}%"
            combined_alert(alert_message)

        if memory_usage > MEMORY_THRESHOLD:
            alert_message = f"High Memory usage detected - {memory_usage}%"
            combined_alert(alert_message)

        time.sleep(10)

monitor_system()
```

This script combines both Slack and email alerts, making it versatile and robust for critical monitoring.

In this chapter, you learned how to set up automated system monitoring and alerts to track server performance and detect issues. We explored how to monitor CPU, memory, and disk usage, filter logs for errors, and send notifications through Slack and email. These tools provide a proactive approach to system management, helping you respond quickly to potential issues. In the next chapter, we'll explore advanced scheduling techniques, such as using cron jobs and task schedulers, to automate scripts and processes across different platforms.

CHAPTER 17: AUTOMATING IMAGE AND VIDEO PROCESSING

Automating image and video processing is useful in many fields, from managing digital assets to creating content for social media. Python provides libraries for editing images, resizing and compressing files, and performing video editing tasks programmatically. In this chapter, we'll explore how to edit images with Pillow, automate image resizing and compression, and handle video processing tasks with MoviePy.

17.1 Editing Images with Pillow

The Pillow library (Python Imaging Library, or PIL) is a powerful tool for image processing. It can handle basic tasks such as cropping, resizing, rotating, and adding text or filters to images, making it ideal for automation.

Setting Up Pillow

Install Pillow with:

bash

pip install pillow

Basic Image Editing Tasks with Pillow

Pillow supports a variety of basic image editing tasks that can be automated to streamline workflows.

Example Recipe: Opening, Rotating, and Saving an Image

This script opens an image file, rotates it by 90 degrees, and saves the rotated image with a new filename.

python

```python
from PIL import Image

# Open an image file
with Image.open("input_image.jpg") as img:
    # Rotate the image
    rotated_img = img.rotate(90)
    # Save the rotated image
```

```
rotated_img.save("rotated_image.jpg")
```

```
print("Image rotated and saved as rotated_image.jpg.")
```

This code opens an image, rotates it by 90 degrees, and saves it under a new filename, making it easy to automate repetitive tasks like rotating or flipping images.

Adding Text to Images

Pillow also allows you to overlay text on images, which can be useful for adding watermarks or creating graphics.

Example Recipe: Adding a Watermark to an Image

python

```python
from PIL import Image, ImageDraw, ImageFont

# Load the image
with Image.open("input_image.jpg") as img:
    # Set up drawing context
    draw = ImageDraw.Draw(img)
    font = ImageFont.truetype("arial.ttf", 36)

    # Add text
    text = "Watermark"
    textwidth, textheight = draw.textsize(text, font)
    width, height = img.size
```

x, y = width - textwidth - 10, height - textheight - 10

draw.text((x, y), text, font=font, fill=(255, 255, 255, 128)) # RGBA for semi-transparent white

Save the watermarked image

img.save("watermarked_image.jpg")

print("Watermark added and image saved as watermarked_image.jpg.")

This script adds a semi-transparent watermark to the bottom right corner of the image.

17.2 Automating Image Resizing and Compression

Resizing and compressing images are common tasks for web optimization and saving storage space. Automating these tasks with Pillow can be a time-saver, especially when handling large batches of images.

Resizing Images

Automating resizing is useful for creating thumbnails, optimizing images for web, or standardizing dimensions for a collection of images.

Example Recipe: Batch Resizing Images

python

```python
import os
from PIL import Image

# Directory containing images
input_folder = "images/"
output_folder = "resized_images/"
os.makedirs(output_folder, exist_ok=True)

def resize_image(image_path, output_path, size=(800, 800)):
    with Image.open(image_path) as img:
        img = img.resize(size, Image.ANTIALIAS)
        img.save(output_path)

# Resize all images in the folder
for filename in os.listdir(input_folder):
    if filename.endswith((".jpg", ".png")):
        resize_image(
            os.path.join(input_folder, filename),
            os.path.join(output_folder, filename),
        )

print("All images resized and saved in", output_folder)
```

This script resizes all images in a specified folder to 800x800 pixels and saves them to a new folder.

Compressing Images

Compressing images reduces file size, which is essential for web and mobile applications.

Example Recipe: Compressing Images

python

```python
def compress_image(input_path, output_path, quality=60):
    with Image.open(input_path) as img:
        img.save(output_path, "JPEG", quality=quality)


# Compress all images in the folder
for filename in os.listdir(input_folder):
    if filename.endswith(".jpg"):
        compress_image(
            os.path.join(input_folder, filename),
            os.path.join(output_folder, filename),
        )
```

print("All images compressed and saved in", output_folder)

This script compresses all JPEG images in a folder by reducing their quality to 60%, effectively reducing file sizes for faster load times.

17.3 Automating Video Editing Tasks with MoviePy

MoviePy is a Python library for video editing, allowing you to automate tasks like trimming, adding text, merging videos, and applying effects. This library is highly useful for creating promotional videos, compiling clips, or adding intros and outros to videos.

Setting Up MoviePy

Install MoviePy with:

bash

```
pip install moviepy
```

Basic Video Editing with MoviePy

MoviePy can perform basic video editing tasks such as cutting clips, adding text overlays, and merging multiple video files.

Example Recipe: Trimming a Video

This script trims a section from a video and saves it as a new file.

python

```
from moviepy.editor import VideoFileClip

# Load video
clip = VideoFileClip("input_video.mp4")
```

```
# Trim the video (from 10 to 20 seconds)
trimmed_clip = clip.subclip(10, 20)
```

```
# Save the trimmed clip
trimmed_clip.write_videofile("trimmed_video.mp4",
codec="libx264")
```

```
print("Video trimmed and saved as trimmed_video.mp4.")
```

This script loads a video, extracts a segment from 10 to 20 seconds, and saves it as a new file. You can modify the subclip() time values as needed.

Adding Text Overlays to Videos

MoviePy can overlay text onto videos, which is useful for adding titles, captions, or watermarks.

Example Recipe: Adding a Title to a Video

python

```
from     moviepy.editor     import     VideoFileClip,     TextClip,
CompositeVideoClip
```

```
# Load video
clip = VideoFileClip("input_video.mp4")
```

```
# Create text clip
```

```python
txt_clip = TextClip("Welcome to My Channel", fontsize=70,
color="white")
txt_clip = txt_clip.set_position("center").set_duration(5)

# Overlay text on video
video = CompositeVideoClip([clip, txt_clip])

# Save the video with overlay
video.write_videofile("video_with_text.mp4", codec="libx264")

print("Text overlay added and saved as video_with_text.mp4.")
```

This script adds a title overlay to the video for the first 5 seconds and then saves it. You can adjust the text, position, and duration to fit your requirements.

Merging Multiple Videos

MoviePy allows you to concatenate multiple video clips into a single video file, which is useful for compiling footage or creating a playlist.

Example Recipe: Merging Video Clips

python

```python
from moviepy.editor import VideoFileClip, concatenate_videoclips

# Load video clips
```

```python
clip1 = VideoFileClip("video1.mp4")
clip2 = VideoFileClip("video2.mp4")
clip3 = VideoFileClip("video3.mp4")

# Concatenate clips
final_clip = concatenate_videoclips([clip1, clip2, clip3])

# Save the final video
final_clip.write_videofile("merged_video.mp4", codec="libx264")

print("Videos merged and saved as merged_video.mp4.")
```

This script concatenates three video clips into one video, saving it as a single file.

Automating Video Compression

Compressing videos is important for managing storage space and optimizing load times for web and mobile applications.

Example Recipe: Compressing a Video

python

```python
def compress_video(input_path, output_path, target_size=20):
    clip = VideoFileClip(input_path)

    # Adjust bitrate based on target size (MB)
    duration = clip.duration  # in seconds
```

```
bitrate = (target_size * 8192) / duration  # convert to kbps
```

```
# Write video with specified bitrate
clip.write_videofile(output_path,          codec="libx264",
bitrate=f"{int(bitrate)}k")
```

```
compress_video("input_video.mp4",  "compressed_video.mp4",
target_size=20)
```

This script compresses a video to a target file size in MB by calculating the appropriate bitrate. Adjust the target_size as needed to manage file size requirements.

In this chapter, you learned how to automate image and video processing tasks using Python. We explored basic image editing with Pillow, including resizing, compressing, and adding watermarks. For video, we used MoviePy to perform tasks like trimming, adding text, merging clips, and compressing files. These tools provide efficient ways to manage multimedia content, making it easy to create consistent, high-quality images and videos for personal or professional use. In the next chapter, we'll delve into automating data scraping from websites, gathering information, and preparing it for analysis or reporting.

CHAPTER 18: BUILDING CLI TOOLS FOR QUICK AUTOMATIONS

Command-line interface (CLI) tools are highly efficient for automating tasks quickly and can be used directly from the terminal, making them ideal for repetitive workflows. With Python, building CLI tools is straightforward and powerful, allowing you to create flexible scripts that perform everything from file management to data processing. This chapter covers the basics of building CLI tools, creating custom tools for repeated tasks, and packaging and distributing these tools for broader use.

18.1 Basics of Building Command-Line Tools

A CLI tool in Python typically involves using libraries like argparse to handle user input and execute commands based on arguments provided. You can develop CLI tools for tasks as varied as file processing, data transformation, or automation.

Setting Up a Basic CLI Tool with argparse

The argparse library allows you to specify arguments for your tool, define options, and manage flags, making it easy to customize the tool's behavior from the command line.

Example Recipe: Basic CLI Tool for Greeting Users

This simple CLI tool accepts a user's name and an optional greeting message.

```python
python


import argparse


# Set up argument parser
parser = argparse.ArgumentParser(description="Greet a user with a message.")
parser.add_argument("name", type=str, help="The name of the user")
```

```
parser.add_argument("-g", "--greeting", type=str, default="Hello",
help="Greeting message")
```

```
# Parse arguments
args = parser.parse_args()
```

```
# Print greeting message
print(f"{args.greeting}, {args.name}!")
```

How to Run: Save this script as greet.py and run it from the command line:

bash

python greet.py Alice -g "Hi"

This command outputs Hi, Alice!. The argparse library lets you add as many arguments and options as needed to customize the tool's behavior.

18.2 Creating Custom CLI Tools for Repeated Tasks

For repeated tasks, creating CLI tools can save significant time, especially when working with tasks like file processing, data manipulation, or system administration. This section covers examples of custom CLI tools for common automation tasks.

File Management CLI Tool

A file management tool can automate tasks like moving, copying, and deleting files, making it useful for organizing directories or managing backups.

Example Recipe: CLI Tool for Moving Files

This tool moves files from one directory to another based on user input.

python

```
import argparse
import os
import shutil

# Set up argument parser
parser = argparse.ArgumentParser(description="Move files from one directory to another.")
parser.add_argument("source", type=str, help="The source directory path")
parser.add_argument("destination", type=str, help="The destination directory path")
parser.add_argument("-e", "--extension", type=str, help="Only move files with a specific extension")

args = parser.parse_args()
```

```python
# Function to move files
def move_files(source, destination, extension=None):
    os.makedirs(destination, exist_ok=True)
    for filename in os.listdir(source):
        if extension and not filename.endswith(extension):
            continue
        source_path = os.path.join(source, filename)
        dest_path = os.path.join(destination, filename)
        shutil.move(source_path, dest_path)
        print(f"Moved: {filename}")


# Execute the function
move_files(args.source, args.destination, args.extension)
```

How to Run: Save this script as file_mover.py and run it as follows:

bash

```bash
python file_mover.py /path/to/source /path/to/destination -e .jpg
```

This command moves all .jpg files from the source directory to the destination directory.

Data Processing CLI Tool

A data processing tool can handle tasks like filtering, transforming, and aggregating data. For example, a tool that reads a CSV file and performs filtering can save time in data analysis workflows.

Example Recipe: CLI Tool for Filtering a CSV File

This tool filters a CSV file based on a specified column and value.

python

```python
import argparse
import pandas as pd

# Set up argument parser
parser = argparse.ArgumentParser(description="Filter a CSV file by a column value.")
parser.add_argument("input_file", type=str, help="Path to the input CSV file")
parser.add_argument("output_file", type=str, help="Path to save the filtered CSV file")
parser.add_argument("column", type=str, help="Column to filter by")
parser.add_argument("value", type=str, help="Value to filter by")

args = parser.parse_args()

# Filter CSV file
def filter_csv(input_file, output_file, column, value):
    df = pd.read_csv(input_file)
    filtered_df = df[df[column] == value]
```

```
filtered_df.to_csv(output_file, index=False)
print(f"Filtered data saved to {output_file}")
```

filter_csv(args.input_file,   args.output_file,   args.column,
args.value)

How to Run: Save this script as filter_csv.py and run it as follows:

bash

python filter_csv.py data.csv filtered_data.csv Status Active

This command filters data.csv for rows where the Status column
has the value Active and saves the result to filtered_data.csv.

18.3 Packaging and Distributing CLI Tools

Distributing your CLI tool allows others to install and use it easily.
Packaging involves structuring the code for distribution, creating
setup files, and uploading it to PyPI if you want it to be publicly
available.

Structuring a CLI Tool for Distribution

Organize your code by creating a directory with an entry-point
script and a setup.py file.

Example Directory Structure:

arduino

mycli_tool/

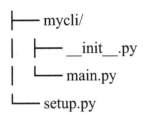

```
├── mycli/
│   ├── __init__.py
│   └── main.py
└── setup.py
```

main.py: This file contains the main logic for your CLI tool. For example, let's use the greeting tool:

python

```python
# mycli/main.py
import argparse

def main():
    parser = argparse.ArgumentParser(description="Greet a user with a message.")
    parser.add_argument("name", type=str, help="The name of the user")
    parser.add_argument("-g", "--greeting", type=str, default="Hello", help="Greeting message")

    args = parser.parse_args()
    print(f"{args.greeting}, {args.name}!")
```

setup.py: This file is used to define the package and entry point for the CLI tool.

python

```python
# setup.py
from setuptools import setup, find_packages

setup(
    name="mycli_tool",
    version="0.1",
    packages=find_packages(),
    entry_points={
        "console_scripts": [
            "greet=mycli.main:main",
        ],
    },
    install_requires=[],
    author="Your Name",
    description="A simple CLI tool to greet users",
)
```

This setup configuration specifies that the tool can be run from the command line using the greet command, which will invoke the main() function in mycli/main.py.

Installing and Testing the CLI Tool Locally

1. Install the tool locally in editable mode:

    bash

pip install -e .

2. Run the CLI tool:

bash

greet Alice -g "Hi"

This command should print Hi, Alice! if the tool is correctly installed.

Publishing the Tool to PyPI

To make the CLI tool available for public use, you can publish it to PyPI.

1. **Create a PyPI account** at https://pypi.org/.
2. **Install twine** for uploading:

bash

pip install twine

3. **Build the package**:

bash

python setup.py sdist bdist_wheel

4. **Upload to PyPI**:

bash

twine upload dist/*

Once uploaded, anyone can install your CLI tool with pip install mycli_tool and use it from the command line.

In this chapter, you learned how to create CLI tools in Python, enabling efficient task automation from the command line. We covered the basics of building CLI tools with argparse, creating custom tools for file management and data processing, and packaging CLI tools for distribution. Packaging and sharing your CLI tools makes them more accessible and useful for a broader audience. In the next chapter, we'll explore how to integrate APIs to further expand the capabilities of your CLI tools, enabling interactions with web services and external data sources.

CHAPTER 19: AUTOMATING NETWORK AND SECURITY TASKS

Automating network diagnostics and security tasks can help streamline troubleshooting, enhance security management, and simplify the configuration of VPNs and proxies. Network and security automation are essential in large IT environments, as they allow for quick detection of issues, performance monitoring, and consistent security practices. This chapter covers automating network diagnostics (like ping and traceroute), scripting basic security tasks, and automating VPN and proxy settings.

19.1 Automating Network Diagnostics (Ping, Traceroute)

Network diagnostics tools like ping and traceroute are fundamental for troubleshooting network issues. Automating these tasks with Python enables continuous monitoring and the ability to quickly identify connection problems.

Automating Ping Requests

The ping command checks if a network device is reachable and measures round-trip time. Automating ping requests allows for periodic checks on the availability of critical network resources.

Example Recipe: Automated Ping Check

This script sends a ping to a specified IP address or domain at regular intervals and logs the results.

python

```
import os
import time

def ping_host(host, interval=5):
```

```
while True:
    response = os.system(f"ping -c 1 {host} > /dev/null 2>&1")  #
'-c 1' for Linux/Mac; use '-n 1' for Windows
    if response == 0:
        print(f"{host} is reachable.")
    else:
        print(f"{host} is not reachable.")
    time.sleep(interval)
```

```
# Example usage
ping_host("google.com", interval=10)
```

This script pings google.com every 10 seconds and prints whether the host is reachable. Adjust the interval as needed.

Automating Traceroute

Traceroute helps identify the path packets take to reach a destination. Automating traceroute checks provides insight into network routing and helps pinpoint where connectivity issues might occur.

Example Recipe: Automated Traceroute Script

python

```
import os
```

```
def traceroute_host(host):
```

```python
print(f"Tracing route to {host}...\n")
os.system(f"traceroute {host}")  # Use 'tracert' on Windows
```

```python
# Example usage
traceroute_host("google.com")
```

This script runs traceroute on a specified host and prints the results. On Windows, replace traceroute with tracert.

19.2 Basic Scripting for Security Tasks

Automating basic security tasks, such as scanning ports or checking for open connections, can help ensure a secure environment. Python provides libraries like socket and subprocess that can be used to automate these checks.

Port Scanning

Port scanning is a way to check for open ports on a machine. Automating port scans can help detect potential vulnerabilities by identifying services that should or shouldn't be exposed.

Example Recipe: Simple Port Scanner

This script checks if specific ports are open on a given host.

python

```python
import socket

def scan_ports(host, ports):
```

```
    print(f"Scanning ports on {host}...")
    for port in ports:
        sock              =              socket.socket(socket.AF_INET,
socket.SOCK_STREAM)
        sock.settimeout(1)
        result = sock.connect_ex((host, port))
        if result == 0:
            print(f"Port {port}: Open")
        else:
            print(f"Port {port}: Closed")
        sock.close()


# Example usage
scan_ports("127.0.0.1", [22, 80, 443, 8080])
```

This script scans a list of ports (22, 80, 443, and 8080) on a specified host and prints whether each port is open or closed.

Checking for Open Network Connections

Automating the check for open network connections can help detect unauthorized connections or unusual activity.

Example Recipe: Checking Open Connections

This script lists active connections, filtering for specific criteria if needed.

python

```
import os

def check_open_connections():
    print("Checking open network connections...")
    os.system("netstat -ant")  # Use 'netstat -an' on Windows

check_open_connections()
```

This script uses netstat to list active network connections and their statuses. On Windows, you may need to use netstat -an.

19.3 Automating VPN and Proxy Settings

VPNs and proxies are essential for securing network traffic and managing access. Automating VPN and proxy configurations can streamline workflows and ensure consistency in network security policies.

Automating VPN Connections

Python can interface with VPN clients, allowing you to connect or disconnect automatically based on your security requirements. This example assumes OpenVPN is installed and configured with .ovpn files.

Example Recipe: Automating VPN Connection with OpenVPN

python

```python
import subprocess
import time

def connect_vpn(vpn_config_path):
    try:
        print("Connecting to VPN...")
        vpn_process = subprocess.Popen(["openvpn", "--config", vpn_config_path])
        time.sleep(5)  # Give some time for the VPN to connect
        print("VPN connected.")
        return vpn_process
    except Exception as e:
        print("Failed to connect to VPN:", e)

def disconnect_vpn(vpn_process):
    if vpn_process:
        vpn_process.terminate()
        print("VPN disconnected.")

# Example usage
vpn_process = connect_vpn("/path/to/your/config.ovpn")
# Disconnect after some time
time.sleep(60)
disconnect_vpn(vpn_process)
```

This script uses OpenVPN to connect to a VPN specified by a configuration file. The VPN connection will be maintained for 60 seconds and then disconnected.

Automating Proxy Configuration

Automating proxy settings can be helpful when you need to route traffic through specific proxies, especially for web scraping or accessing restricted content. This example demonstrates changing proxy settings for a Python application.

Example Recipe: Setting Up a Proxy for HTTP Requests

This script configures HTTP and HTTPS proxies in a Python script, allowing it to route web requests through the specified proxy.

python

```python
import requests

def fetch_with_proxy(url, proxy):
    proxies = {
        "http": f"http://{proxy}",
        "https": f"https://{proxy}"
    }
    try:
        response = requests.get(url, proxies=proxies)
        print(f"Status Code: {response.status_code}")
```

```
    print(response.text[:500])   # Print the first 500 characters of
the response
    except Exception as e:
      print("Failed to fetch the URL through proxy:", e)
```

```
# Example usage
proxy = "proxy_ip:proxy_port"  # Replace with your proxy IP and
port
fetch_with_proxy("http://example.com", proxy)
```

This code configures the requests library to use a proxy for HTTP and HTTPS requests, allowing controlled access to external sites via the specified proxy.

Automating Proxy Settings System-Wide (Linux)

On Linux systems, proxy settings can be configured globally by exporting environment variables.

Example Recipe: Setting System-Wide Proxy in a Script

bash

```
#!/bin/bash
```

```
# Set system-wide proxy
export http_proxy="http://proxy_ip:proxy_port"
export https_proxy="http://proxy_ip:proxy_port"
```

```
# Run a network task through the proxy
curl http://example.com
```

This Bash script sets environment variables for http_proxy and https_proxy, applying proxy settings to all commands run within the session. Save it as set_proxy.sh and run it with bash set_proxy.sh.

In this chapter, we explored automating network and security tasks using Python. We covered how to automate network diagnostics like ping and traceroute, basic security checks like port scanning and open connection monitoring, and the automation of VPN and proxy configurations. These tools can greatly enhance network management and security monitoring by simplifying routine tasks and providing consistent, reliable results. In the next chapter, we'll dive into automating data retrieval and processing from web APIs, integrating various online services to expand the functionality of our scripts.

CHAPTER 20: INTEGRATING PYTHON WITH IOT DEVICES

The Internet of Things (IoT) connects physical devices to the internet, enabling control, automation, and data collection from a wide range of smart devices. Python, with its wide variety of libraries and compatibility with microcontrollers, is an excellent language for working with IoT devices, making it easy to automate smart home tasks and collect data from various sensors. This chapter covers controlling IoT devices with Python, automating smart home tasks, and collecting and processing data from IoT devices.

20.1 Controlling IoT Devices with Python

Python can interact with IoT devices using communication protocols like HTTP, MQTT, and WebSocket. Many IoT platforms provide APIs that Python can use to send commands or receive updates from devices.

Using MQTT to Control IoT Devices

MQTT (Message Queuing Telemetry Transport) is a lightweight protocol commonly used for IoT because of its low power and bandwidth requirements. paho-mqtt is a popular Python library for connecting to MQTT brokers.

Example Recipe: Controlling a Smart Bulb via MQTT

This example assumes a smart bulb connected to an MQTT broker, where you can publish commands to control its state.

1. Install paho-mqtt:

bash

pip install paho-mqtt

2. Use the following script to send commands to the bulb.

python

```python
import paho.mqtt.client as mqtt

# Define MQTT broker and topic
broker = "mqtt_broker_address"
port = 1883
topic = "home/livingroom/bulb"

# Connect to the MQTT broker and publish a command
def control_smart_bulb(command):
    client = mqtt.Client()
    client.connect(broker, port)
    client.loop_start()
    client.publish(topic, command)
    client.loop_stop()
    client.disconnect()
    print(f"Sent command: {command}")

# Example usage
```

control_smart_bulb("ON") # Turn the bulb on

control_smart_bulb("OFF") # Turn the bulb off

This script connects to an MQTT broker and sends an ON or OFF command to the smart bulb topic.

Using HTTP APIs for IoT Device Control

Many IoT devices can be controlled via HTTP APIs, allowing you to send commands directly over the network. For example, some smart thermostats and lights offer RESTful APIs.

Example Recipe: Controlling a Smart Thermostat via HTTP

This example sends a command to adjust the temperature on a smart thermostat.

python

```
import requests

# API endpoint and token
api_url = "http://thermostat_ip/api/v1/temperature"
api_token = "your_api_token"

def set_temperature(value):
    headers = {"Authorization": f"Bearer {api_token}"}
    data = {"temperature": value}
    response = requests.post(api_url, json=data, headers=headers)
```

```
if response.status_code == 200:
    print(f"Temperature set to {value}°C.")
else:
    print("Failed to set temperature:", response.status_code)
```

```
# Example usage
set_temperature(22)  # Set temperature to 22°C
```

This code sends a POST request to the thermostat's API to set the temperature. Adjust the api_url and api_token based on your device's configuration.

20.2 Automating Smart Home Tasks

Python can help you automate smart home tasks by scheduling commands or triggering actions based on specific conditions. Libraries like schedule and datetime enable you to create automated routines that manage lighting, climate, and security devices.

Scheduling Tasks with schedule

The schedule library allows you to set timed tasks, such as turning off lights at night or activating home security systems in the evening.

Example Recipe: Automating Smart Lights with a Daily Schedule

1. Install schedule:

bash

```
pip install schedule
```

2. Use the following code to schedule light control.

python

```
import paho.mqtt.client as mqtt
import schedule
import time

broker = "mqtt_broker_address"
port = 1883
topic = "home/livingroom/light"

def turn_on_light():
    client = mqtt.Client()
    client.connect(broker, port)
    client.loop_start()
    client.publish(topic, "ON")
    client.loop_stop()
    client.disconnect()
    print("Light turned on.")

def turn_off_light():
```

```
client = mqtt.Client()
client.connect(broker, port)
client.loop_start()
client.publish(topic, "OFF")
client.loop_stop()
client.disconnect()
print("Light turned off.")


# Schedule light automation
schedule.every().day.at("18:00").do(turn_on_light)   # Turn on at
6:00 PM
schedule.every().day.at("23:00").do(turn_off_light)   # Turn off at
11:00 PM


# Run scheduled tasks
while True:
    schedule.run_pending()
    time.sleep(60)
```

This script turns the light on at 6:00 PM and off at 11:00 PM every day. You can customize the timing and add more tasks to fit your needs.

Triggering Actions Based on Sensor Data

Automations can also be triggered by sensor data, such as motion or temperature readings. The following example automates fan control based on a temperature sensor reading.

Example Recipe: Automating Fan Based on Temperature

This example periodically reads temperature data and turns on a fan if the temperature exceeds a threshold.

python

```python
import requests
import time

temp_sensor_url = "http://sensor_ip/api/v1/temperature"
fan_topic = "home/livingroom/fan"
broker = "mqtt_broker_address"
port = 1883
temp_threshold = 25  # Temperature threshold in °C

def control_fan(status):
    client = mqtt.Client()
    client.connect(broker, port)
    client.loop_start()
    client.publish(fan_topic, status)
    client.loop_stop()
    client.disconnect()
    print(f"Fan turned {status.lower()}.")

# Check temperature and control fan
```

```python
while True:
    response = requests.get(temp_sensor_url)
    if response.status_code == 200:
        temperature = response.json()["temperature"]
        print(f"Current temperature: {temperature}°C")

        if temperature > temp_threshold:
            control_fan("ON")
        else:
            control_fan("OFF")
    time.sleep(60)  # Check every minute
```

This script checks the temperature every minute and turns on the fan if the temperature exceeds 25°C, or off if it's below.

20.3 Collecting and Processing Data from IoT Devices

Collecting data from IoT devices can provide valuable insights for monitoring, troubleshooting, and optimizing home automation. Python can aggregate data from devices like temperature sensors, humidity sensors, and cameras, enabling data analysis and visualization.

Collecting Sensor Data for Analysis

Collecting and storing data from IoT sensors can help you analyze trends, such as temperature fluctuations, over time.

Example Recipe: Logging Temperature Data

This script logs temperature data from a sensor every 10 minutes and saves it to a CSV file.

python

```python
import requests
import csv
import time
from datetime import datetime

sensor_url = "http://sensor_ip/api/v1/temperature"
log_file = "temperature_log.csv"

# Initialize CSV file with headers
with open(log_file, "w", newline="") as file:
    writer = csv.writer(file)
    writer.writerow(["Timestamp", "Temperature"])

# Log temperature data periodically
while True:
    response = requests.get(sensor_url)
    if response.status_code == 200:
        temperature = response.json()["temperature"]
        timestamp       =       datetime.now().strftime("%Y-%m-%d
%H:%M:%S")
```

```python
# Log data to CSV
with open(log_file, "a", newline="") as file:
    writer = csv.writer(file)
    writer.writerow([timestamp, temperature])

    print(f"Logged temperature: {temperature}°C at {timestamp}")
    time.sleep(600)  # Log every 10 minutes
```

This script retrieves temperature data from a sensor every 10 minutes, logs it to a CSV file, and prints the current reading.

Visualizing IoT Data

Visualizing collected data can help identify trends and monitor the performance of smart home systems. Libraries like matplotlib can be used to plot data for better insights.

Example Recipe: Plotting Temperature Data

This script loads temperature data from a CSV file and plots it using matplotlib.

python

```python
import pandas as pd
import matplotlib.pyplot as plt

# Load data from CSV
```

```python
data                =                pd.read_csv("temperature_log.csv",
parse_dates=["Timestamp"])
data.set_index("Timestamp", inplace=True)

# Plot temperature over time
plt.figure(figsize=(10, 6))
plt.plot(data.index, data["Temperature"], marker="o")
plt.title("Temperature over Time")
plt.xlabel("Time")
plt.ylabel("Temperature (°C)")
plt.grid()
plt.show()
```

This code reads temperature data from temperature_log.csv and plots it, showing how temperature has changed over time.

In this chapter, you learned how to integrate Python with IoT devices, making it possible to control devices, automate smart home tasks, and collect data for analysis. We explored controlling devices using MQTT and HTTP, scheduling tasks like light automation, triggering actions based on sensor readings, and visualizing data from sensors. In the next chapter, we'll look at how to use Python to handle machine learning models and automate data analysis, enabling smart decision-making for IoT applications and other use cases.

CHAPTER 21: ADVANCED API AUTOMATION

APIs are essential for automating workflows across various online services, allowing seamless integration between applications like Slack, Zoom, Google, and more. Automating these workflows enables tasks like scheduling meetings, sending notifications, managing documents, and processing data without manual intervention. This chapter covers automating workflows with popular APIs, handling authentication with OAuth, and building end-to-end API-based workflows.

21.1 Automating Workflows with Popular APIs (Slack, Zoom)

Many popular platforms provide APIs that allow developers to interact with them programmatically, enabling the automation of common workflows. Two of the most frequently used APIs are Slack (for communication) and Zoom (for video conferencing).

Automating Slack Notifications

Slack's API enables the automation of notifications, making it easy to send messages to specific channels or users. To interact with the Slack API, you need a Slack Bot Token, which can be obtained by creating a Slack App and adding it to your workspace.

Example Recipe: Sending Automated Messages to Slack

1. Create a Slack App at api.slack.com/apps.
2. Add the app to a workspace, and grant it the necessary permissions (e.g., chat

).

3. Use the following code to send a message to a Slack channel.

python

```
import requests

# Slack API URL and Bot Token
slack_url = "https://slack.com/api/chat.postMessage"
token = "xoxb-your-slack-bot-token"   # Replace with your bot token
channel = "#general"  # Replace with the target channel

def send_slack_message(message):
    headers = {"Authorization": f'Bearer {token}"}
    data = {
        "channel": channel,
        "text": message
    }
    response = requests.post(slack_url, headers=headers, json=data)
    if response.status_code == 200 and response.json().get("ok"):
        print("Message sent to Slack successfully.")
    else:
        print("Failed to send message:", response.json())
```

Example usage

send_slack_message("Hello from Python! This message was automated.")

This code sends a message to the specified Slack channel. Customize the channel and token variables based on your configuration.

Automating Zoom Meeting Scheduling

Zoom's API allows you to schedule meetings, making it easy to automate meeting setup for regular check-ins, appointments, or webinars. You'll need to create a Zoom App with the necessary permissions to use this API.

Example Recipe: Scheduling a Zoom Meeting

1. Go to marketplace.zoom.us and create an app with the appropriate permissions.
2. Obtain an OAuth or JWT token.
3. Use the following script to schedule a meeting.

python

```
import requests
import datetime


# Zoom API endpoint and access token
```

```python
zoom_url = "https://api.zoom.us/v2/users/me/meetings"
access_token = "your_zoom_access_token"  # Replace with your
OAuth or JWT token


def schedule_zoom_meeting(topic, start_time, duration_minutes):
    headers = {"Authorization": f"Bearer {access_token}"}
    data = {
        "topic": topic,
        "type": 2,  # Scheduled meeting
        "start_time": start_time.isoformat(),
        "duration": duration_minutes,
        "timezone": "UTC",
        "settings": {"join_before_host": True}
    }
    response = requests.post(zoom_url, headers=headers, json=data)
    if response.status_code == 201:
        meeting_info = response.json()
        print("Meeting scheduled successfully:", meeting_info)
    else:
        print("Failed to schedule meeting:", response.json())


# Example usage
topic = "Project Sync"
start_time = datetime.datetime.utcnow() + datetime.timedelta(days=1)  # 1 day from now
```

schedule_zoom_meeting(topic, start_time, 30)

This script schedules a meeting on Zoom for the specified topic, start time, and duration. Customize access_token with your own token.

21.2 Using OAuth and Token Management

OAuth is an authentication protocol commonly used by APIs to grant access without sharing passwords. In OAuth-based authentication, a user grants access to an application by authorizing it, and the application receives a temporary access token for API requests.

OAuth 2.0 Flow

OAuth 2.0 generally follows these steps:

1. The application redirects the user to an authorization URL.
2. The user grants access, and the API returns an authorization code.
3. The application exchanges the authorization code for an access token.
4. The application uses the access token for API requests.

Implementing OAuth 2.0 with the Requests Library

This example demonstrates how to obtain an access token for Google's APIs, allowing the application to access Google Calendar data on behalf of the user.

1. Register your application on Google Developer Console and obtain client credentials.
2. Use the following script to complete the OAuth flow and request calendar data.

Example Recipe: Google OAuth 2.0 Authentication for API Access

python

```
import requests
import webbrowser

client_id = "your_client_id"
client_secret = "your_client_secret"
redirect_uri = "http://localhost"  # For testing on localhost
scope = "https://www.googleapis.com/auth/calendar.readonly"

# Step 1: Get authorization code
auth_url = f"https://accounts.google.com/o/oauth2/v2/auth?client_id={client_id}&redirect_uri={redirect_uri}&scope={scope}&response_type=code&access_type=offline"
webbrowser.open(auth_url)
auth_code = input("Enter the authorization code from the browser: ")
```

```python
# Step 2: Exchange authorization code for access token
token_url = "https://oauth2.googleapis.com/token"
data = {
    "client_id": client_id,
    "client_secret": client_secret,
    "code": auth_code,
    "grant_type": "authorization_code",
    "redirect_uri": redirect_uri
}
response = requests.post(token_url, data=data)
tokens = response.json()
access_token = tokens.get("access_token")


# Step 3: Use access token to make API requests
calendar_url = "https://www.googleapis.com/calendar/v3/users/me/calendarList"
headers = {"Authorization": f"Bearer {access_token}"}
response = requests.get(calendar_url, headers=headers)
if response.status_code == 200:
    calendar_data = response.json()
    print("Calendar data:", calendar_data)
else:
    print("Failed to retrieve calendar data:", response.json())
```

This script performs the OAuth flow for Google's Calendar API, allowing you to access calendar data with the acquired access token.

21.3 Building End-to-End Automated API Workflows

End-to-end automation across multiple APIs allows you to connect workflows between platforms, achieving complex automation sequences. For example, you might integrate Slack and Zoom to send automated Slack messages with Zoom meeting links, or Google Calendar and email to automatically notify attendees.

Building a Workflow: Scheduling a Zoom Meeting and Sending a Slack Notification

This example automates a workflow that schedules a Zoom meeting and sends the meeting link to a Slack channel.

python

```
import requests
import datetime


# Slack and Zoom configuration
slack_token = "your_slack_token"
slack_channel = "#general"
zoom_token = "your_zoom_token"


# Step 1: Schedule a Zoom meeting
```

```python
def schedule_zoom_meeting(topic, start_time, duration_minutes):
    zoom_url = "https://api.zoom.us/v2/users/me/meetings"
    headers = {"Authorization": f"Bearer {zoom_token}"}
    data = {
        "topic": topic,
        "type": 2,
        "start_time": start_time.isoformat(),
        "duration": duration_minutes,
        "timezone": "UTC",
        "settings": {"join_before_host": True}
    }
    response = requests.post(zoom_url, headers=headers, json=data)
    if response.status_code == 201:
        return response.json()["join_url"]
    else:
        print("Failed to schedule meeting:", response.json())
        return None


# Step 2: Send a Slack message with the Zoom meeting link
def send_slack_message(message):
    slack_url = "https://slack.com/api/chat.postMessage"
    headers = {"Authorization": f"Bearer {slack_token}"}
    data = {
        "channel": slack_channel,
        "text": message
```

```
}
response = requests.post(slack_url, headers=headers, json=data)
if response.status_code == 200 and response.json().get("ok"):
    print("Message sent to Slack successfully.")
else:
    print("Failed to send message:", response.json())


# Combine steps: Schedule meeting and send Slack notification
topic = "Team Sync"
start_time          =          datetime.datetime.utcnow()          +
datetime.timedelta(days=1)
duration = 30
meeting_url = schedule_zoom_meeting(topic, start_time, duration)


if meeting_url:
    slack_message = f"A new Zoom meeting has been scheduled:
{meeting_url}"
    send_slack_message(slack_message)
```

This workflow schedules a meeting on Zoom and then sends the meeting link to a Slack channel, automating an entire workflow from scheduling to notification.

In this chapter, you learned how to use APIs to automate workflows with popular services like Slack and Zoom, implement OAuth 2.0 for secure access to APIs, and build end-to-end workflows that connect multiple platforms. These skills enable you to streamline communication, scheduling, and task management in integrated environments, making it possible to handle complex automation across different applications. In the next chapter, we'll delve into automating machine learning workflows, from training models to deploying them, bringing automation to data science and AI applications.

CHAPTER 22: BRINGING IT ALL TOGETHER: BUILDING AN AUTOMATION PORTFOLIO

Now that you have explored various automation techniques, it's time to bring everything together into a cohesive portfolio that showcases your expertise. A well-organized automation portfolio demonstrates your ability to streamline tasks, optimize processes, and build solutions for a range of applications. This chapter covers how to organize and document your automation projects, best practices for maintaining scripts, and the next steps for scaling and deploying automation solutions.

22.1 Organizing and Documenting Automation Projects

An organized portfolio is essential for sharing your work with others, showcasing your skills, and maintaining consistency across projects. By grouping projects by category, adding documentation, and providing clear instructions, you make it easy for others to understand and use your solutions.

Structuring Your Portfolio

A well-structured portfolio should contain separate folders for each project, clear naming conventions, and organized code. Here's an example folder structure:

markdown

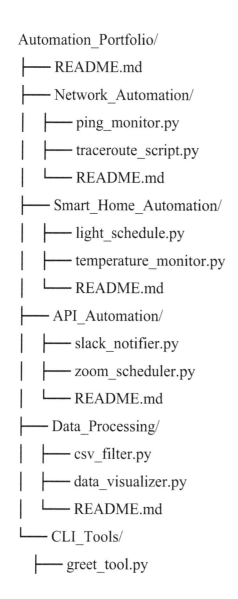

```
Automation_Portfolio/
├── README.md
├── Network_Automation/
│   ├── ping_monitor.py
│   ├── traceroute_script.py
│   └── README.md
├── Smart_Home_Automation/
│   ├── light_schedule.py
│   ├── temperature_monitor.py
│   └── README.md
├── API_Automation/
│   ├── slack_notifier.py
│   ├── zoom_scheduler.py
│   └── README.md
├── Data_Processing/
│   ├── csv_filter.py
│   ├── data_visualizer.py
│   └── README.md
└── CLI_Tools/
    ├── greet_tool.py
```

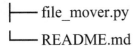 file_mover.py

└── README.md

Each project folder contains its own README.md file, explaining the purpose, usage, dependencies, and configuration steps for the project. The main README.md at the root level provides an overview of the entire portfolio.

Writing Effective Documentation

Documenting each project is critical for making it usable and understandable. Here are some elements to include in each README.md:

1. **Project Title and Description**: Briefly describe the project and its purpose.

2. **Installation Instructions**: List any dependencies and how to install them.

3. **Configuration**: Provide instructions for setting up configurations like API keys, paths, or environment variables.

4. **Usage**: Include examples of how to run the script and any command-line arguments.

5. **Output**: Show sample output or results to set expectations.

6. **Troubleshooting**: Address common issues or solutions for setup and usage.

Example README.md for light_schedule.py (Smart Home Automation):

markdown

Light Schedule Automation

Description
This script automates a daily schedule to turn lights on and off in a smart home environment using MQTT.

Installation
- Install dependencies:
  ```bash
  pip install paho-mqtt schedule
  ```

CONFIGURATION

- Update the broker variable with the IP address of your MQTT broker.
- Set the topic for your smart light device.

USAGE

To run the light schedule:

bash

```
python light_schedule.py
```

The lights will turn on at 6:00 PM and off at 11:00 PM every day.

TROUBLESHOOTING

- Ensure the MQTT broker is running and accessible.
- Check that the topic matches the device configuration.

yaml

Documentation like this makes it easy for others to understand your code and replicate your automation.

22.2 Best Practices for Maintaining Automation Scripts

Maintaining automation scripts requires regular updates, testing, and refactoring to ensure they continue working effectively as dependencies, APIs, and environments change.

Version Control with Git

Using Git for version control allows you to track changes, manage branches for new features, and collaborate with others. GitHub or

GitLab can host your automation portfolio, allowing others to view, fork, and contribute to your projects.

1. **Initialize a Git repository** in your portfolio directory:
   ```bash
   git init
   ```

2. **Commit and push** changes regularly:

   bash

   ```
   git add .
   git commit -m "Initial commit"
   git push origin main
   ```

Setting Up Testing and Validation

Automation scripts benefit from testing, especially when handling critical or repetitive tasks. Unit tests ensure each function performs as expected, while integration tests validate workflows across different components.

1. **Unit Testing**: Test individual functions or modules.
   - Use unittest or pytest for creating automated test cases.
   - Example:

     python

```python
import unittest
from light_schedule import turn_on_light


class TestLightSchedule(unittest.TestCase):
    def test_turn_on_light(self):
        result = turn_on_light()
        self.assertEqual(result, "Light turned on.")


if __name__ == "__main__":
    unittest.main()
```

2. **Continuous Integration (CI)**: Set up a CI pipeline on GitHub Actions, GitLab CI, or another CI/CD service to automatically run tests on every commit.

Using Virtual Environments and Dependency Management

A virtual environment isolates each project's dependencies, preventing conflicts between versions of libraries. Use requirements.txt to specify dependencies and make it easy for others to set up the environment.

1. **Create a virtual environment**:

bash

```bash
python -m venv venv
```

2. **Activate the virtual environment**:

bash

```
source venv/bin/activate  # On macOS/Linux
venv\Scripts\activate     # On Windows
```

3. **Freeze dependencies**:

bash

```
pip freeze > requirements.txt
```

Users can then install the exact dependencies with:

bash

```
pip install -r requirements.txt
```

22.3 Next Steps: Scaling and Deploying Automation Solutions

As you gain experience with automation, you may want to scale up your solutions, deploy them to servers, or even turn them into services used by others. Here are some next steps for scaling and deploying automation solutions.

Deploying Automation Scripts to the Cloud

Cloud services like AWS, Azure, and Google Cloud can run automation scripts on virtual machines, allowing for scaling and remote access.

1. **Amazon EC2 or Google Cloud VM**: Deploy scripts to a virtual machine to run continuously or on a schedule.

2. **AWS Lambda or Google Cloud Functions**: Use serverless functions to run lightweight automation without maintaining infrastructure.

3. **Docker**: Containerize your projects with Docker, making it easy to deploy across different environments.

Example: Running light_schedule.py on AWS Lambda with an MQTT dependency packaged in a Docker container for an isolated runtime environment.

Scheduling with Cloud-Based Tools

For automation workflows that need to run at specific intervals, cloud scheduling tools can simplify and streamline the process.

- **AWS EventBridge** (formerly CloudWatch Events) or **Google Cloud Scheduler** can trigger scripts or APIs at set intervals, ideal for tasks like sending daily reports or performing scheduled backups.

Building Automation APIs for Reusable Services

Turn automation solutions into APIs so others can trigger them remotely. Frameworks like Flask or FastAPI allow you to quickly build and deploy APIs that interface with your automation scripts.

Example Recipe: Exposing a Slack Notification Script as an API with Flask

1. Install Flask:

   bash

   pip install Flask

2. Create a simple Flask app:

   python

   ```python
   from flask import Flask, request, jsonify
   import requests

   app = Flask(__name__)

   @app.route("/notify", methods=["POST"])
   def notify():
       message = request.json.get("message")
       slack_token = "your_slack_token"
       slack_url = "https://slack.com/api/chat.postMessage"
   ```

```python
    headers = {"Authorization": f"Bearer {slack_token}"}
    data = {"channel": "#general", "text": message}
    response = requests.post(slack_url, headers=headers,
json=data)
    return jsonify(response.json())


if __name__ == "__main__":
    app.run(debug=True)
```

This Flask app exposes an endpoint (/notify) to send a message to Slack. It can be deployed on a server and called from other services or scripts.

This final chapter brought together the skills and techniques you've learned throughout the book to help you create a polished automation portfolio. We covered how to organize and document your projects, maintain them effectively with best practices, and scale your solutions using cloud infrastructure and APIs. As you continue building automation projects, you'll be able to develop more complex, integrated systems that can streamline workflows, enhance productivity, and even offer solutions to a wider audience. Congratulations on completing this journey through Python automation!

www.ingramcontent.com/pod-product-compliance
Lightning Source LLC
LaVergne TN
LVHW051443050326
832903LV00030BD/3218